Loved having you
here.
L. Bacall /AKA
Mary Martin

Me, too, Jeffrey Van Slant

Wake Up and Smell the Coffee

Laura Zahn

Down to Earth Publications
St. Paul, Minnesota

Other books by Laura Zahn:

"Room at the Inn/Minnesota - Guide to Minnesota's Historic B&Bs, Hotels and Country Inns"
"Room at the Inn/Wisconsin - Guide to Wisconsin's Historic B&Bs and Country Inns"
"Ride Guide to the Historic Alaska Railroad," with Anita Williams.

To Mom,

Mary Elizabeth Day Zahn,

for Mom's apple pie,

Mom's Christmas cookies, Mom's cinnamon rolls, et al.

For
Iva Davidson Day, Eva Cole Zahn,
Jessie Doubleday Davidson, Rosa Pearl Paine
and
all the generations of my family's foremothers
who spent much of their lives in early kitchens
on Midwest farms, in small towns, even in a lumber camp,
cooking and canning and baking,
to sustain and nourish us through the years
to today,
when cooking can be simply a pleasure,
and clean up's a breeze.

Published by **Down to Earth Publications**
1426 Sheldon Street
St. Paul, Minnesota 55108

Distributed by **Voyageur Press**
123 North Second Street
Stillwater, Minnesota 55082
1-800-888-9653 or 612-430-2210

ISBN 0-939301-03-2

Library of Congress Cataloging in Publication Data

Zahn, Laura C., 1957-
            Wake Up and Smell the Coffee.
            Includes index.

1. Breakfasts   2. Cookery   3. Bed and Breakfast Accommodations - Middle West - Directories

TX 733.Z3   88-71538

Dewey System - Ideas and Recipes for Breakfast and Brunch - 641.52

Cover Illustration by Lynn Fellman, Golden Valley, Minnesota

Map by Jim Miller, St. Paul, Minnesota

Typography of contents: Apple MacIntosh MacWrite and LaserWriter Plus printer

Printing by Malloy Lithographing, Ann Arbor, Michigan

3 4 5 6 7 8 9 10

Many thanks to Lynn Fellman, Tom and Helene,
Kathy O'Neill, Mary Zahn, EZ Finance,
April Bernard, Kristina Ford, Sylvia Morse
and my handsome husband, Jim Miller.

Special thanks to the innkeepers
for sharing their best recipes and artwork,
for their cooking hints and ideas,
and for their enthusiasm and encouragement.

I also thank them for the privilege
of being the "middleperson" in communicating their favorite recipes
to many hungry cooks and readers.

Introduction

Say "Bed and Breakfast" three times fast (or even three times not so fast) and your tongue may find itself saying, *"Bread* and Breakfast." Perhaps it's no mistake.

Here in the Midwest, the morning repast -- and sometimes afternoon tea, evening social hour or bedtime snack, as well -- at the small inns and guest houses known as "B&Bs" often accounts for the most memorable part of the visit (or at least deserves more than second billing). Rarely does an innkeeper here set out plain old bacon and eggs or, heaven forbid, cold cereal and toast (you can get that at home if, indeed, there's time or interest in morning food at all). Breakfast at many Midwest B&B inns is a special event, like the getaway itself.

In our toaster-pastry/breakfast-sandwich society, it is heartening to hear that breakfast -- a real meal, that is -- is making a comeback, at least on weekends. We've long heard that breakfast is the most important meal of the day, providing fuel to ensure good mental and physical performance all day long. But another trend -- the increasing interest in good home cookin' from the Heartland -- is helping to make breakfast more popular. "Slow foods," trend-setters apparently have noticed, nourish the soul as well as the body through their aroma, texture and taste. More people are bypassing diet and convenience foods for "real" food that's substantial and satisfying.

And that, in the proverbial nutshell, is breakfast. No other meal has the comforting aromas of breakfast. Smells are carried more acutely and accurately in our memories than any of our other senses. It seems each of us carries around a scent storage file that's suddenly flung open to reveal a time and place we'd long since tucked away. The whiff of a campfire, or even a fireplace, always sends me back to hot dogs and s'mores, sappy songs and mosquitoes around a fire at summer camp. And what adult Midwesterner can't say that the smell of a fall leaf pile or (now only in some small and remote communities) the smell of burning leaves brings back a flash of childish romps in raked leaves, hands blistered from raking, or crisp, clear autumn days?

Overnights at B&Bs with home-cooked breakfasts are sure to create new favorite aroma "files." Here, in these big homes, guests really do "Wake Up and Smell the Coffee." And the Streusel Coffeecake. And the Pumpkin Pancakes. And the Hot Apple Crisp.

As I traveled in Minnesota and Wisconsin to write my "Room at the Inn" B&B guidebooks, I found that wonderful, mouth-watering smells waft up from the kitchen, creep silently up the stairway, slip under doorways and through the quilts to the noses of slumbering guests. And don't just take my word for it. Here's what some innkeepers shared:

"Our back stairs lead to the four guest bedrooms on the second floor. A sure way to get our guests stirring is to open the door and let the fragrance of the morning special rise and gently intrude upon a blissful slumber," wrote Bill Cecil of the Scofield House, Sturgeon Bay, Wis.

"Our guests don't have to worry about getting up on time," said Ruth Leibner of Greystone Farms, East Troy, Wis. "We always give them our special wake-up call. When the coffee is done brewing, the bacon and sausages sizzling and the tantalizing smell of fresh-baked apple cake, cinnamon rolls or coffeecake have built up in the kitchen, all we do is open the kitchen door leading to the dining room. The aroma quickly finds its way through the parlors and up the open staircase to our sleeping guests. Works every time!"

"The mouth-watering aroma of the baking Sour Cream-Cinnamon Breakfast Cake eliminates any need for an alarm clock!" wrote Penny Shaw of the Bridge Street Inn in Charlevoix, Mich.

And from Lois Barrot of Country B&B in Shafer, Minn.: "If the roosters don't wake you up, I guarantee the coffee will!"

Only B&B inns small enough so that guests can smell breakfast cooking were invited to participate in this cookbook. Their brand of hospitality is, indeed, very different from larger operations.

And that's why this is more than a cookbook. In order to get more of the "flavor" of the inn and innkeeper from whom the recipe came, information about the people and place is included underneath each recipe. If you're more than an arm-chair traveler, do try to visit the inns that sound appealing to you. Their addresses and phone numbers are listed so you can contact them for more information, and a map is included to give you an idea of their locations.

Every B&B is unique. That's the beauty of them. Likewise, every B&B breakfast is different. These recipes, however, share an affinity for "from-scratch" cooking, with a short-cut here and there. In general, they are for quantities reasonable for home use. Most are surprisingly simple to follow. Several can be prepared ahead of time.

Most innkeepers encouraged creativity in adapting these recipes. As you read them, you'll discover many already have improved on great basic ideas (for instance, isn't Dessert for Breakfast long overdue?). And the food certainly is not limited to consumption only at breakfast or brunch -- after all, "pancake suppers" are a Midwest tradition, too!

Like a well-loved teddybear who is missing an eye and perhaps has lost a little stuffing over the years, in time this cookbook will display, I hope, the smears and sprinkles that mean it has been pulled off the shelf and used again and again.

Contents

Preserves, Butters, Spreads and Sauces

Fruits

Entrees

See also, continued:

Other Favorites

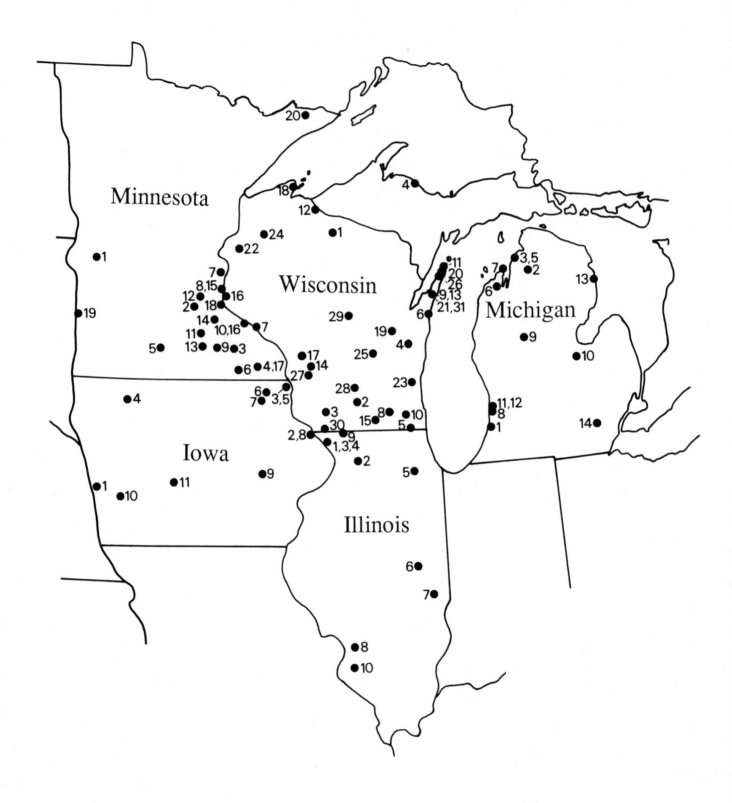

MINNESOTA

1. American House, Morris
2. Bluff Creek Inn, Chaska
3. Canterbury Inn, Rochester
4. Carrolton Country Inn, Lanesboro
5. Cedar Knoll Farm, Good Thunder
6. Chase's, Spring Valley
7. Country Bed & Breakfast, Shafer
8. Driscoll's For Guests, Stillwater
9. Eden B&B, Dodge Center
10. Evergreen Knoll Acres, Lake City
11. Hutchinson House, Faribault
12. Linné, Minneapolis
13. Northrop House, Owatonna
14. Quill & Quilt, Cannon Falls
15. Rivertown Inn, Stillwater
16. Red Gables Inn, Lake City
17. Scanlan House, Lanesboro
18. Thorwood, Hastings
19. Triple L Farm, Hendricks
20. Young's Island, Gunflint Trail/Grand Marais

WISCONSIN

1. Chippewa Lodge, Lac du Flambeau
2. Collins House, Madison
3. Duke House, Mineral Point
4. The Farm Homestead, New Holstein
5. Foxmoor B&B, Wilmot
6. The Gables, Kewaunee
7. Gallery House, Alma
8. Greene House B&B, Whitewater
9. Gray Goose, Sturgeon Bay
10. Greystone Farms, East Troy
11. Griffin Inn, Ellison Bay
12. The Inn, Montreal
13. Inn at Cedar Crossing, Sturgeon Bay
14. Inn at Wildcat Mountain, Ontario
15. Jackson Street Inn, Janesville
16. Jefferson-Day House, Hudson
17. Just-N-Trails, Sparta
18. Old Rittenhouse Inn, Bayfield
19. The Parkside, Appleton
20. Renaissance Inn, Sister Bay
21. Scofield House, Sturgeon Bay
22. Seven Pines Lodge, Lewis
23. Stagecoach Inn, Cedarburg
24. The Stout Trout B&B, Springbrook
25. Strawberry Hill B&B, Green Lake
26. Thorp House Inn, Fish Creek
27. Trillium, LaFarge
28. Victorian Treasure, Lodi
29. Victorian Swan on Water, Stevens Point
30. Wisconsin House Stagecoach Inn, Hazel Green
31. White Lace Inn, Sturgeon Bay

MICHIGAN

1. A Country Place, South Haven
2. Arman House, Boyne Falls
3. Bay B&B, Charlevoix
4. Big Bay Point Lighthouse B&B, Big Bay
5. Bridge Street Inn, Charlevoix
6. Hillside B&B, Cedar (Traverse City)
7. Hutchinson's Garden, Northport
8. Kirby House, Saugatuck
9. Lynch's Dream, Evart
10. Montague Inn, Saginaw
11. Old Holland Inn, Holland
12. The Parsonage 1908, Holland
13. Silver Creek B&B, Black River
14. Urban Retreat, Ann Arbor

IOWA

1. Apple Orchard Inn, Missouri Valley
2. Collier Mansion, Dubuque
3. FitzGerald's Inn, Lansing
4. Hannah Marie Country Inn, Spencer
5. Lansing House, Lansing
6. Montgomery Mansion, Decorah
7. Old World Inn, Spillville
8. Redstone Inn, Dubuque
9. Rettig House, Middle Amana
10. Victorian B&B Inn, Avoca
11. Walden Acres, Adel

ILLINOIS

1. Avery Guest House, Galena
2. Barber House Inn, Polo
3. Belle Aire Mansion, Galena
4. Comfort Guest House, Galena
5. Die Blaue Gans, Naperville
6. Grandma Joan's Homestay, Champaign
7. Inn on the Square, Oakland
8. Maggie's Place, Collinsville
9. Noni's B&B, Warren
10. Westerfield House, Freeburg

Things You Should Know

> Please read the entire recipe before beginning to find out how hot to preheat the oven, what size pan(s) to grease, or how many hours or days ahead of time the recipe must be started.

> Baking and cooking temperatures are listed in Fahrenheit.

> Remember to preheat the oven to the temperature listed in the recipe before baking.

> Assume that white (granulated) sugar is called for in these recipes when the ingredients list "sugar." Powdered (confectioner's) or brown sugar is listed as such.

> Brown sugar usually is "packed" into the measuring cup, not loose.

> When making yeast breads or preserves, read the yeast or pectin package instructions thoroughly. For yeast breads, preserves and recipes which involve canning, you may wish to consult a cookbook with detailed instructions for these processes.

> Recipes have been listed in chapters according to the way in which innkeepers serve them. For instance, you will find some fruit dishes in chapters other than "Fruits," and dishes that could be suitable as "Dessert for Breakfast" are included in other chapters because the innkeepers serve them as snacks, holiday fare or even entrees. The table of contents, therefore, also is an index so you can double-check other chapters at a glance.

> While the format of the recipes has been standardized, the recipes remain in the words of the innkeepers as much as possible. Innkeepers had the opportunity to double-check their recipes before printing.

> Most innkeepers encouraged experimentation with their recipes, such as substituting or adding ingredients for personal preferences or health reasons. Many of these recipes, they said, were devised through their own experimentation with a basic recipe.

When eating out, you find breakfast beverage selections often limited to coffee, one kind of tea, or orange or tomato juice. B&Bs break all the rules for the morning eye-opener, rules that were meant to be broken long ago. Some innkeepers' ideas are so simple that there is no recipe, such as stirring a little peach schnapps into orange juice, or adding cinnamon or almond-flavored liqueur to morning coffee. Read on for their more elaborate suggestions. And *why not* enjoy a fresh strawberry daiquiri before breakfast? Or egg nog in the "off-season?"

Beverages

Cider to Sit Around With

Ingredients:

Apple cider
1/4 that amount of cranberry juice
1/2 dozen cinnamon sticks
2 tablespoons whole cloves

> Stir desired amount of cider together in saucepan with 1/4 that amount of cranberry juice.
> Heat together with cinnamon sticks and cloves.
> Serve in a "coffee keeper" that will keep it hot for a long time.

from **Driscoll's for Guests**
1103 South Third Street
Stillwater, Minnesota 55083
612-439-7486

"This makes the whole house smell like a holiday," said Innkeeper Mina Driscoll. The hot cider is especially welcomed by autumn and winter guests to charming Stillwater, the birthplace of Minnesota, only a half-hour drive from Minneapolis and St. Paul. Guests come to stroll along the historic main street and stop in renovated shops and restaurants. The downtown is situated on and below the steep limestone bluffs carved by the St. Croix River, which pleasure boaters enjoy in the summer.

Mina serves the steaming brew for afternoon tea after guests check in. It's designed "to sit around with," probably in the parlor in front of her fireplace or while someone's playing the parlor piano.

Her B&B is in one of Stillwater's oldest homes. The original rosewood, pine and walnut woodwork, carefully carved by Swedish carpenters who worked without blueprints, still remains throughout the home. The three guest-rooms are decorated with family antiques, reproductions, wicker and other "country" and Victorian furnishings.

Other Driscoll's for Guests recipes:
Pumpkin Poundcake, page 83
Oo-Hoo's Strawberry-Rhubarb Jam, page 100

Spiced Cider Glog

Ingredients:

1 quart cranberry juice
3 quarts apple cider
1 to 2 cups brandy
1/2 cup brown sugar
3 broken cinnamon sticks
Orange peel - either in strips or 2 teaspoons, grated
12 whole cloves
Dash of nutmeg

> Mix first four ingredients together in a 36-cup party percolator.
> Combine cinnamon sticks, orange peel, cloves and nutmeg. Place either in cheesecloth and drop into the brew, or line the percolator basket with filter and place mixture in filter.
> Percolate and serve hot, either alone or with cinnamon sticks.

Makes about 32 four-ounce servings

from **The Scofield House**
908 Michigan Street
Sturgeon Bay, Wisconsin 54235
414-743-7727

"Fran and I argue over the timing for adding the brandy," said Innkeeper Bill Cecil, who, with Fran, his wife, opted for a career change and now put their decision-making skills from the health care field to good use in the Scofield House kitchen. "When added before the glog is perked, the alcohol is cooked off. I prefer to add it after the perking cycle is complete."

Cross-country skiers enjoying Door County's trails enjoy this aprés-ski glog either way. Inside this 1902 home, they can sip glog by the fireplace while marveling at the incredible woodwork. Built by the owner of what was once Wisconsin's biggest hardware store, the house has oak carved walls, ceiling and stairway and a remarkable inlaid hardwood floor.

The Cecils put a great deal of work into the rest of the house (including 68 gallons of paint on the exterior) before opening in the summer of 1987. Now, guests can choose from four upstairs guest-rooms. And, in between sips of glog, they can pound out a tune on the upright piano in the parlor or use a telescope to examine the skies over Door County and Lake Michigan.

Another Scofield House recipe:
Carrot Bran Muffins, page 48

Candlelight Coffee for Two

Ingredients:

    1 ounce Grand Marnier liqueur
    Hot, strong coffee (French roast preferred)
    1 tablespoon coffee-flavored liqueur
    Whipped cream

> Heat the Grand Marnier over a fondue burner in a heat-proof cup until it flames, about 1-1/2 minutes, slightly touching the flame to the liqueur.
> Add hot, strong coffee. Top with whipped cream.
> Pour coffee-flavored liqueur in a metal tablespoon. Heat over the fondue burner, letting the liqueur catch the flame.
> Drizzle the flaming coffee liqueur over the whipped cream.
> Repeat with the second cup.

from **Bluff Creek Inn**
1161 Bluff Creek Drive
Chaska, Minnesota 55318
612-445-2735

What could be more romantic than a flaming coffee drink on a cold winter night? "Spectacular presentation!" said Innkeeper Anne Karels, who makes this special coffee for couples who come to this country B&B for getaways. And there's no reason it can't be done easily at home, she added.

Anne's love for cooking started just the opposite -- at home, and then moved to the B&B business. Her family members "were happy to try different things and were very quick to give pats on the back." That led to lots of entertaining, and in mid-1988, the purchase of the inn, a renovated five guest-room farmhouse located a half hour from the Twin Cities.

Having her own inn was her dream, since she had decided it was a good way to combine her business, "people" and culinary skills. "In fact, when my last employer asked in an interview what my long-term goals were, I told him I intended to own and operate a B&B within five years. Never did I dream that less than a year later I would be the innkeeper at Bluff Creek Inn!" Anne is keeping the tradition of a huge, elegant breakfast at Bluff Creek, and the hors d'oeuvres and wine in the evenings. A new offering is couples' packages, including cooking your own gourmet dinner at a new cooking school on a nearby farm, where Anne is an assistant instructor.

Other Bluff Creek Inn recipes:
Stuffed Baked Apples, page 103
Special Valentine Meringues, page 189

Swedish Egg Coffee

Ingredients:

    20 cups cold water
    16 tablespoons regular grind coffee
    1 egg

> Measure water into an enamel coffee pot and bring to boiling.
> Measure ground coffee into mixing bowl. Add raw egg and mix well.
> Add coffee-egg mixture to boiling water. Turn down the burner and stir well with a long wooden spoon.
> Simmer coffee for two minutes, then boil hard one minute.
> Let the coffee rest for one minute, then pour 1/4 cup cold water into the coffee to settle the grounds.
> Strain into a "coffee keeper" or favorite pot.

Makes 20 cups

from **Country Bed and Breakfast**
32030 Ranch Trail
Shafer, Minnesota 55074
612-257-4773

"The coffee is fragrant and has a rich, clear amber color and tastes wonderful," said Lois Barott. "My grandmother always served this coffee for special occasions and neighborhood 'coffee parties.' Then my mother carried on her tradition. I started to drink coffee at a young age -- it was a special treat. So I was taught to make Swedish Egg Coffee and I am carrying on the tradition."

Lois grew up in the 1882 brick farmhouse built by a Swedish immigrant, one of many who settled in the Shafer, Lindstrom and Chisago Lakes area. She and Budd, her husband, raised their six children here. When the house seemed too big and the 69-mile commute to work in the Twin Cities became too far, they decided to renovate and open their home as a B&B.

The three guest-rooms are upstairs with wicker and antique furniture. Lois has sewn the comforters. Downstairs, she and Budd serve this coffee to guests who sit around the kitchen table as Barotts prepare breakfast.

This farm B&B is located on a quiet country road just right for a stroll. Cats, ducks, chickens and a friendly dog are the remaining farm animals. Pepper's biggest thrill is a guest who throws sticks for him to retrieve. The scenic St. Croix River and canoeing and boat rides are five miles away.

Strawberry Daiquiri

Ingredients:

    1 cup fresh strawberries
    2 tablespoons frozen limeade concentrate
    1 cup crushed ice
    1 to 2 one-ounce jiggers white rum
    2 tablespoons sugar (omit if using frozen berries)

> Combine all ingredients in a blender. Blend until smooth and thick.

Makes 2 servings

from **Strawberry Hill B&B**
Route 1, Box 524-D
Green Lake, Wisconsin 54941
414-294-3450

What else should start breakfast at Strawberry Hill B&B? Innkeeper Patricia Spencer grows her own strawberries right outside the kitchen door, and the dining room wallpaper and strawberry motif dishes bring the patch indoors for guests who are visiting in the winter.

"This is a wonderfully decadent replacement for the traditional orange juice," she said. "It is the house specialty and all breakfasts begin with a Strawberry Daiquiri, followed by fresh fruit of the season and selected entrees." Unused portions, she said, may be left in the blender or frozen in a separate container. Frozen berries can be used if fresh are unavailable.

Pat opened her four guest-room B&B in 1986. Originally from the area, she returned after living in California to work as a busy, full-time volunteer for the Heifer Project, an established interfaith agency that provides farm animals to farmers in developing countries. "I really didn't know what I'd do at the end of that year," she said. "I saw this house and I had to have it." Redecorating was all that was necessary to convert the farmhouse to a B&B.

Guests especially appreciate the hot tub on the glassed-in sun porch, from which the strawberry patch, the barn and surrounding fields can be seen.

Other Strawberry Hill recipes:
Bauernfruhstuck, page 147
Christmas or Easter Danish, page 180

Homemade Egg Nog

Ingredients:

1/2 teaspoon vanilla
4 large eggs, separated
4 tablespoons raw honey, divided
4 cups whole milk
1/2 teaspoon salt

Also:

Nutmeg for sprinkling

> Beat yolks with 2 tablespoons honey in a small bowl.
> In a double-boiler, heat milk to 180 degrees.
> *Slowly* pour milk into egg yolk mixture.
> Return mixture to double boiler and heat again to 180 degrees. Stir often (this will cook into a thin custard that coats the spoon). Then cool thoroughly.
> In separate bowl, beat egg whites until very stiff.
> Beat in other 2 tablespoons of honey and the vanilla.
> When custard mixture has cooled, carefully stir in egg white mixture. Add salt and stir thoroughly.
> Chill at least two hours before serving.

Makes 2 quarts

from **Trillium**
Route 2, Box 121
LaFarge, Wisconsin 54639
608-625-4492

"This is a true family favorite any season of the year because it is just as refreshing in warm weather as it is appropriate during the winter holiday season," said Rosanne Boyett. "Here on the farm, there is always a plentiful supply of fresh eggs and milk. We like it best when sprinkled lightly with nutmeg just as it is served." Guests may find a pitcher of Egg Nog in her guest house refrigerator, along with Amish cheese and the farm's eggs.

You might not think you can "wake up and smell" breakfast cooking in a separate guest house. But Rosanne bakes fresh bread every day, and guests who are out for an early morning walk can tell. And when Rosanne arrives at the doorstep with fresh, hot muffins and bread, the cozy cottage is quickly filled with the aroma. This guest house is set on an 85-acre farm in the heart of Wisconsin's Amish country. Guests can visit with the lambs, calves and chickens, climb into the treehouse, or hike in the hilly woods. Or they simply can relax in front of the fireplace.

Mary's Elbows

Ingredients:

    1/2 banana
    1/2 cup frozen orange juice concentrate
    1/4 cup sour cream
    1/2 teaspoon nutmeg
    1/2 cup water
    1/2 cup crushed ice

> Put all ingredients except the ice into a blender and blend well.
> Add 1/2 cup crushed ice.
> Serve at once.

Makes 2-4 servings, depending on size of the glass

from **Hannah Marie
Country Inn**
**Route 1, Highway 71 South
Spencer, Iowa 51301
712-262-1286**

Innkeeper Mary Nichols and husband Ray named this beverage one hectic morning after she had concocted a new breakfast drink when some ingredients had been overlooked on the grocery list and she was up to her elbows in dishwater. Since there's a cocktail called "Mary's Knees," the name stuck, and now there is a tradition that guests toast Mary's elbows before drinking this drink. This orange juice beverage in a goblet greets guests in the morning. They enjoy it in an antique rocker or porch swing.

"For an afternoon refresher when guests arrive after a long drive, we will very often serve this with an added 1 cup Seven Up," said Mary. "It's quite nice served in the library-game room."

Mary is a retired California home economics teacher who came home to Iowa to open her own inn in a farmhouse a few miles from where her mother, Hannah Marie, was born. The restored 1910 home now is known for its romantic rooms done in a country-Victorian decor. It's also gaining a reputation for theme teas in the afternoons, such as "Tea with the Mad Hatter" on Saturdays or ethnic teas most weekdays.

Other Hannah Marie Country Inn recipes:
Three Pepper Frittata, page 152
Naughty Torte, page 209

Summer Sherbet Tea

Ingredients:

   1 pint lemon, lime, orange or other favorite sherbet, 3/4 of which has been softened
   1/3 cup instant tea powder
   1 to 2 tablespoons sugar (unnecessary if tea is already sweetened)
   3 cups milk

Also:

   Lemon, lime or orange slices and/or mint sprigs

> Beat softened sherbet, instant tea and sugar with a mixer or blender until smooth.
> Add cold milk. Beat just until foamy.
> Pour into cold glasses. Top with scoops of the remaining sherbet and garnish with fruit slices and/or mint sprigs. Serve immediately.

Makes five 8-ounce servings

from **Carrolton Country Inn**
Route 2, Box 139
Lanesboro, Minnesota 55949
507-467-2257

This cold tea drink is a sparkling refreshment on a hot summer afternoon in the country, served when guests first arrive, said Innkeeper Gloria Ruen. Guests are handed a tall glass either just before or after they receive a house tour and hear the history of the inn.

There's much to see and hear. Guests hear about the scenic Ox Cart Road, the stagecoach route on which they just drove three miles under the tree canopy from Lanesboro. They also hear where the Root River flows through the property (canoes can be rented in town and the river can be canoed 74 miles to the Mississippi) and where the Root River Bike Trail runs across it (this is a popular 10-mile state trail from Fountain to Lanesboro).

And they want to know about the farmhouse, now renovated as a four guest-room inn. Built prior to 1882, it was owned by a Norwegian bachelor farmer for many years. Gloria and Charles, too, lived in it for seven years until their growing family needed the convenience of a paved road closer to town (Gloria comes over to check in the B&B guests, assist them and cook breakfast). Two years of work and 91 gallons of paint stripper went into the project, and those with an interest in historic home restoration can get the straight story here. The inn is decorated in antiques.

Cinnamon and breakfast go together like, well, like chocolate and nuts. And there's enough cinnamon or streusel in many of these tantalizing coffeecakes to rouse anyone with half a sweet-tooth straight out of bed. The best thing about coffeecakes may be that it's socially acceptable to eat them for a first or main course rather than holding off until dessert. Many of these recipes include enough healthful ingredients -- fruit, yogurt and oatmeal, for instance -- so no guilt is necessary, and at least one coffeecake can be stirred up the night before to bake fresh in the morning.

Coffeecakes

Apple Squares

Ingredients:

1 cup sugar
1 cup unsweetened applesauce
1/2 cup butter
2 cups sifted flour
1 teaspoon baking soda
1-1/2 teaspoon cinnamon
1 teaspoon nutmeg
Dash of ground cloves
1/4 teaspoon salt
1 cup raisins
1 cup nuts, chopped
1 teaspoon vanilla

Topping:
3 tablespoons sugar
1 teaspoon cinnamon

> Combine all ingredients. Mix well with a mixer.
> Spread with a rubber spatula onto a greased cookie sheet with edges or jelly roll pan.
> Sprinkle with sugar mixed with cinnamon.
> Bake at 350 degrees until lightly browned, 25-35 minutes.

Makes 24-36 squares

from **The Griffin Inn**
11976 Mink River Road
Ellison Bay, Wisconsin 54210
414-854-4306

"This recipe was given to my mom because she is allergic to eggs. She passed it on to me and it has become a Griffin Inn favorite."

Laurie Roberts' mom has helped Laurie and Jim with their Griffin Inn in more ways than providing recipes. She was the one who called from her Fish Creek home and told them the Griffin Inn was for sale. "We were up four hours later" from Milwaukee, Laurie said, and six weeks later they moved in as the new owners. They had opted for a career change (Jim was a busy hospital administrator) and they were looking for a Door County business to own and run together as their daughters grew up. They'd planned to retire in the area, but the inn brought them up 25 years earlier.

Other Griffin Inn recipes:
Old-Fashioned Oats Coffeecake, page 37
Orange Butter, page 96
Sesame Whole Wheat Pancakes, page 140
Apple-Bacon-Cheddar Bake, page 146

Apple Yogurt Coffeecake

Ingredients:

4 tablespoons butter, melted
4 tablespoons brown sugar
1 teaspoon cinnamon
4 medium apples, cored and sliced
1 cup butter
1 cup sugar
2 eggs
4 cups flour
2 teaspoons baking powder
2 teaspoons baking soda
1/2 teaspoon salt
2 cups plain yogurt

Streusel Filling:
1/2 cup sugar
2 tablespoons butter, melted
2 tablespoons flour
2 teaspoons cinnamon
1/2 cup walnuts or pecans,
    chopped

> Combine melted butter with brown sugar and cinnamon in a 9 x 13-inch pan ("This makes a very high coffeecake."). Smooth evenly over the bottom of the pan.
> Arrange apple slices over the brown sugar mixture.
> Cream butter and sugar. Add eggs, one at a time, beating well after each addition.
> Combine flour, baking powder, soda and salt. Add the dry ingredients to the creamed mixture alternately with yogurt.
> Spread half the batter over the apple slices.
> Mix streusel filling and sprinkle it over the batter in the pan.
> Spread remaining batter over the filling.
> Bake at 350 degrees for 35-40 minutes or until a toothpick inserted in the center comes out clean.
> Remove from oven, invert and slice.

from **The Inn at Cedar Crossing**
336 Louisiana Street
Sturgeon Bay, Wisconsin 54235
414-743-4200

Innkeeper Terry Wulf has a collection of apple recipes so she can serve Door County's bounty to guests right from the orchards September through April. This is a favorite, and when it bakes, the guests upstairs know it.

Other Inn at Cedar Crossing recipes:
Surprise Muffins, page 58
Fresh Rhubarb Bread, page 84
Zucchini Chocolate Nut Bread, page 88
Nectarines with Cream Anglaise, page 113
Hot Apple Crisp, page 192
Crispy Caramel Corn, page 202

Historic Apple Cake

Ingredients:

1 cup honey
1/2 cup sugar
3/4 cup shortening
2 eggs
1 teaspoon baking soda
2-1/2 cups sifted flour
3/4 teaspoon cinnamon
3/4 teaspoon salt
3/4 cup warm coffee
3 or 4 Delicious apples, to make 3 cups diced
1/2 cup walnuts, chopped

Topping:
1/2 teaspoon cinnamon
1/2 cup light brown sugar

> Cream sugar, honey and shortening. Add eggs and beat well.
> Sift together flour, soda, cinnamon and salt. Stir into creamed mixture alternately with coffee.
> Peel, core and dice apples and measure 3 cups.
> Fold apples and nuts into the batter. Pour into a 9 x 13-inch greased pan.
> Combine cinnamon and brown sugar and sprinkle topping over cake batter.
> Bake at 350 degrees for 45 minutes.

from **The Stagecoach Inn
Bed & Breakfast**
**W6I N520 Washington Avenue
Cedarburg, Wisconsin 53012
414-375-0208**

Parts of this recipe were borrowed from an historic Cedarburg cookbook that featured recipes from the past, said Innkeeper Liz Brown. This little town, 20 minutes from Milwaukee, is full of historic buildings and is a 59-building National Historic District. A mill has been converted to shops and restaurants, and a covered bridge, believed to be the last in Wisconsin, is three miles away.

When it comes to history, guests won't find many more authentically restored B&B inns than this one. Liz and Brook, both teachers, took extra time to follow old photos as models and to keep the original layout. The furniture is all antique. Walls of the 12 guest-rooms are stenciled. Plank floors have been stained and softened with rag rugs.

Another Stagecoach Inn B&B recipe:
Cedarburg Apple Muffins, page 44

Berry Cake

Ingredients:

3/4 cup butter or margarine
1-1/2 cups sugar
3 eggs
3 cups flour
1 cup milk
1 teaspoon vanilla
3 teaspoons baking powder
2 cups raspberries, blackberries, blueberries or cut-up strawberries

Also:

Powdered sugar

> Cream butter and sugar.
> Beat eggs and add one at a time.
> Stir in flour alternately with the milk.
> Add vanilla, baking powder and berries last.
> Pour into a greased and floured springform or bundt pan. Bake at 350 degrees for one hour.
> When the cake has cooled, sift powdered sugar on the top.

from **Chippewa Lodge B&B**
3525 Chippewa Lodge Trail
Lac du Flambeau, Wisconsin 54538
715-588-3297

Innkeeper Ann Rayson has been making this cake for 20-some years, starting with the basic cake recipe. "The berries were an inspired addition. We use whatever berries we pick in the woods or sometimes condescend to buy them in the market," she said. "This cake makes breakfast an occasion and goes well with our Kona macadamia nut and chocolate macadamia nut Hawaiian coffees." She and Ben Bess bring the coffees when they come with their three kids to spend the summer at Chippewa Lodge. Ann, now an English professor at the University of Hawaii, has spent summers in this neck of the woods since she was a child. Her marriage to Ben, a regional book publisher, and subsequent motherhood didn't stop that.

In 1983, they bought the former fishing lodge on Ike Walton Lake. It's still the only "commercial" establishment there. They opened four guest-rooms in 1986. The lodge is on the lake, and guests can swim out in front.

Another Chippewa Lodge recipe:
Bran Pancakes, page 132

Blueberry Streusel Coffeecake

Ingredients:

3/4 cup sugar
1/4 cup margarine
1 egg
1/2 cup milk
2 cups flour
2 teaspoons baking powder
1/2 teaspoon salt
2 cups fresh blueberries (or, if frozen, thawed and drained)

Streusel Topping:
1/2 cup sugar
1/3 cup flour
2 teaspoons cinnamon
1/4 cup butter or margarine

> Mix sugar, margarine and egg until creamy. Stir in milk.
> Sift together flour, baking powder and salt. Stir into creamed mixture.
> Gently blend in blueberries. Batter will be firm.
> Pour into an 8 x 8-inch greased and floured pan.
> Sprinkle with streusel topping.
> Bake at 350 degrees for 45-50 minutes or until a toothpick tests clean.

from **A Country Place**
Route 5, Box 43
North Shore Drive
South Haven, Michigan 49090
616-637-5523

"We are located in the heart of the fruit belt and blueberry country," said Innkeeper Lee Niffenegger. "I double the amount of blueberries to two cups as they are so plentiful and so delicious, but the amount can be cut in half and it will still be terrific." Lee has substituted fresh chopped apples or peaches, too, and it works well. "Peach batter should have 1 teaspoon nutmeg added," she advises. Guests like to enjoy this coffeecake on the deck that overlooks Lee and Art's five-and-a-half acres of woods. City folks delight in viewing the birds at the feeder and there's real excitement when the occasional raccoon or deer is sighted.

Lee wanted to open a B&B when she and Art returned from England, where he worked for two years and they "B&B'd" nearly every weekend. After six months of what Lee calls "concentrated renovation with the help of two full-time contractors," A Country Place opened in May 1986.

Other Country Place recipes:
Easy A.M. Cinnamon Rolls, page 72
Hot Cooked Apples, page 104

Cranapple Coffeecake

Ingredients:

3 ounces cream cheese, softened
1/4 cup butter or margarine, softened
2 cups buttermilk biscuit mix
1/3 cup milk

Frosting:
1 cup powdered sugar
4-1/2 teaspoons cranberry juice
1/2 teaspoon vanilla

Filling:
1 quart fresh or frozen
   cranberries
1 orange, peeled and seeded
1-1/2 cups sugar
1 cup apple, peeled and chopped
1 tablespoon sugar
1 tablespoon brown sugar
1/8 teaspoon cinnamon
1/8 teaspoon nutmeg

> Blend cream cheese, butter and biscuit mix with a pastry blender until it resembles coarse meal.
> Add milk and stir with a fork.
> Knead the dough on a floured board until smooth. Roll into a 12 x 18-inch rectangle.
> For the filling, blend the cranberries, orange and sugar in a food processor.
> Stir in the apple, sugars and spices. This will look like a cranberry relish.
> Spoon the relish mixture down the center of the dough.
> With scissors, make a cut 2-l/2 inches deep every inch along both sides. Fold these strips over the filling, alternating sides.
> Bake at 425 degrees for 20 minutes.
> When cool, drizzle with icing made by combining the sugar, cranberry juice and vanilla.

from **The Avery Guest House**
606 South Prospect Street
Galena, Illinois 61036
815-777-3883

This coffeecake is a favorite during the large continental breakfasts guests enjoy in the sunny dining room at Flo and Roger Jensen's Avery Guest House. Their B&B is in one of Galena's spacious historic homes, built in the 1830s on the hillside overlooking the Galena River and remodeled in the 1920s. Guests from any of the four guest-rooms play the piano, engage in a table game in the library, or just sit on the porch swing and enjoy the view.

The Avery Guest House is well within walking distance of downtown, where visitors to this historic community love to stroll in and out of antique, gift and candy shops. Galena has returned nearly all its buildings to their 1800's look, and the town has become a model for restoration efforts.

Danish Kringle

Ingredients:

1/2 cup butter or margarine, chilled
2 cups flour
3 tablespoons sugar
1/2 teaspoon salt
1 package dry yeast
1/4 cup warm water
1 egg
1/2 cup warm milk

Also:

White or cinnamon-flavored icing

Walnut Filling:
3/4 cup walnuts, chopped
1/2 cup brown sugar
1/4 cup margarine, melted
Prune Filling:
3/4 cup pitted prunes
4 tablespoons sugar
1 tablespoon lemon juice
1/2 teaspoon cinnamon

> Cut margarine into flour, sugar and salt in a large bowl until fine crumbs form.
> Dissolve yeast in warm water. Stir yeast, egg and milk into flour mixture and beat until the dough is smooth and soft.
> Cover and refrigerate at least two hours (no longer than 24 hours).
> Divide dough in half (refrigerate other half). Roll dough into a 15 x 6-inch rectangle.
> Spread filling down center of rectangle in a 3-inch strip. Fold sides of dough over filling with a 1-1/2-inch overlap. Pinch edges to seal.
> Arrange kringle on a greased cookie sheet.
> Repeat with other half of dough.
> Let rise in warm place for 30 minutes.
> Bake at 375 degrees for 20-25 minutes. Drizzle with icing when cool, if you choose.
> For Walnut Filling: Simply mix all ingredients.
> Prune Filling: Simmer prunes for 30 minutes in just enough water to cover them. Chop or puree the simmered prunes and add remaining ingredients.

Makes 2 coffeecakes

from **The Rivertown Inn**
306 West Olive Street
Stillwater, Minnesota 55082
612-430-2955

Danish Kringle is one of the dozen or more home-baked pastries on the weekend breakfast buffet at this lumberman's home, now a nine guest-room inn recently renovated by Judy and Chuck Dougherty. Chuck, who does the baking with Judy, recommends a different filling or icing for variety.

Other Rivertown Inn recipes:
Eggs Mornay, page 121
Blueberry Buttermilk Oatmeal Pancakes, page 131
Pumpkin Custard Flan, page 198

Danish Puff Cake

Ingredients:

1 cup butter, half of which is softened
2 cups flour
1 cup and 2 tablespoons cold water
1 teaspoon almond extract
3 eggs

Glaze:
1-1/2 cups powdered sugar
2 tablespoons soft butter
1 teaspoon vanilla
2 tablespoons warm water

Also:

Chopped nuts

> For the basic cake, cut softened butter into 1 cup flour until it is like small peas.
> Sprinkle 2 tablespoons cold water over it and mix to form a ball.
> Divide dough in half. Roll out to two 12 x 3-inch rectangles. Place 3 inches apart on ungreased cookie sheet.
> For the "puff," heat the rest of butter and water to a rolling boil.
> Remove from heat and quickly stir in almond extract and remaining flour. Stir vigorously for about one minute until the mixture forms a ball.
> Cool slightly. Then, beating constantly, add eggs one at a time. Beat until smooth and glossy.
> Spread over the rectangles, covering the dough completely.
> Bake at 350 degrees for one hour until topping is crisp and brown. Cool. The topping will shrink up and fall, forming a "custardy" top.
> Drizzle with a glaze made by mixing the glaze ingredients. Sprinkle with chopped nuts.

Variations - Spread any of the following over the dough before covering with topping:
-Sugar and cinnamon mixture
-Raspberry, strawberry or other favorite jam
-Date, almond, poppyseed or prune canned fillings
-Cream cheese blended with apple butter and a little sugar

from **Greystone Farms B&B**
770 Adam's Church Road
East Troy, Wisconsin 53120
414-495-8485

These folks know "good cookin'." Ruth Leibner and daughter Alane turn out one of the biggest breakfasts in the Midwest, even more than you'd expect a farm B&B breakfast to be. It's served up with plenty of laughter in their beautifully restored turn-of-the-century farm home.

Other Greystone Farms recipes:
Spicy Tomato Jam, page 101
Overnight Pancake Batter, page 137
Fried Tomatoes, page 170

Old-Fashioned Oats Coffeecake

Ingredients:

2 cups flour
2 teaspoons baking powder
1/2 teaspoon salt
2/3 cup old-fashioned rolled oats
3 tablespoons sugar
1/2 teaspoon cinnamon
1 egg
1-1/4 cups milk
1/4 cup vegetable oil

Streusel Topping and Filling:
2/3 cup brown sugar
2/3 cup old-fashioned oats
1/4 cup butter, melted
1/2 cup nuts
1/2 teaspoon cinnamon

> Mix the dry ingredients. In another bowl, combine the egg, milk and oil.
> Combine all. Pour half of the batter into a greased 9 x 9-inch pan.
> Top with half of the streusel mixture.
> Pour on the other half of the batter, then top with remaining streusel.
> Bake at 350 degrees for 35-40 minutes.

from **The Griffin Inn**
11976 Mink River Road
Ellison Bay, Wisconsin 54210
414-854-4306

Somewhere in Nevada, a bakery probably is selling this coffeecake right now. Laurie Roberts sold a Griffin Inn cookbook with this recipe to a guest from Nevada, and a friend of hers soon obtained the recipe for her bakery.

It would be nice to have a taste of the Griffin Inn in Nevada, but even nicer to be up in Door County savoring it first-person. Laurie and Jim ring the breakfast bell at 8:30 and guests assemble at long tables for a long breakfast, it always turns out, because everyone gets to talking. Chances are, guests have already met the evening before over a bowl of popcorn shared around the fireplace. This is another chance to swap suggestions with other area visitors on the best restaurants, shops, beaches, fish boils and perches from which to watch the sunset.

Other Griffin Inn recipes:
Apple Squares, page 29
Orange Butter, page 96
Sesame Whole Wheat Pancakes, page 140
Apple-Bacon-Cheddar Bake, page 146

Overnight Coffeecake

Ingredients:

2 cups flour
1 teaspoon baking powder
1 teaspoon baking soda
1 teaspoon cinnamon
1/2 teaspoon salt
1 cup sugar
2/3 cup butter or margarine
1/2 cup brown sugar
2 eggs
1 cup buttermilk
1 cup drained or chopped raw fruit, optional

Topping:
1/2 cup brown sugar
1/2 cup nuts, chopped
1 teaspoon cinnamon
Optional:
1/4 teaspoon nutmeg

> Mix all dry ingredients in a large mixing bowl.
> Add all remaining ingredients. Pour into a greased 9 x 13-inch pan.
> Mix the topping ingredients. Sprinkle over the batter.
> Cover the pan and refrigerate overnight.
> The next day, set the pan out on the counter while preheating oven to 350 degrees.
> Bake 45-50 minutes. Turn off the oven, open the oven door and let the coffeecake cool in the oven. Cut it into squares and serve while warm.

Makes 16 squares

from **The Gables**
821 Dodge Street
Kewaunee, Wisconsin 54216
414-388-0220

"I add fruit to this coffeecake -- anything in season," said Penny Dunbar. "Since I'm trying to serve Wisconsin products, I add red tart cherries, blueberries or apples. This is so easy for those rushed days. And the aroma while baking wakes up anyone's appetite!"

Guests will find locally-made fruit coolers are served with appetizers upon arrival. Penny, a microwave food instructor, has found a way to combine her three-microwave kitchen and considerable cooking talents with her own brand of hospitality at this B&B. Her husband, Earl, practically stumbled on this beautiful 1885 house while on a sales call in Kewaunee, though the 22-room Queen Anne Victorian was in need of much loving restoration. They opened their B&B in June 1987 and have four guest-rooms upstairs.

Other Gables recipes:
Christmas Scent, page 175
Breakfast Fruit Delight, page 183

Mother's Fresh Rhubarb Cake

Ingredients:
   1/2 cup shortening
   1-1/2 cups sugar
   1 egg
   2 cups flour
   1 teaspoon baking soda
   Dash of salt
   1 cup buttermilk
   1 teaspoon vanilla
   2 cups fresh rhubarb (or apples, coarsely chopped

Also:
   Sugar, cinnamon and broken nuts

> Sift together flour, soda and salt.
> Mix shortening, sugar and egg and beat well. Mix in vanilla.
> Add flour mixture alternately with the buttermilk, beginning and ending with flour.
> Fold the rhubarb into the batter.
> Pour into a well-greased 9 x 13-inch pan or two 8 x 8-inch pans.
> Sprinkle generously with sugar, cinnamon and nuts.
> Bake at 350 degrees for 30-35 minutes or until "toothpick test is positive" (that is, it comes out clean from middle of the cake).

from **The Inn at**
Wildcat Mountain
Highway 33
Ontario, Wisconsin 54651
608-337-4352

Patricia and Wendell Barnes bought this B&B on the banks of the Kickapoo River in early 1988, and it gives Patricia the chance to use many of her skills, especially cooking. "I cook by ear and rarely make a dish the same way twice," she said. But she promises this recipe of her mother's is one she's made so often she could do it in her sleep. "It's wonderful with morning coffee or tea, warm or cold," she said.

Breakfast is served here in the dining room or on the front porch in the summer. Guests can choose from two or three homebaked items, such as this coffeecake, plus Wisconsin cheeses, fresh fruit, yogurt and cereal.

Other Inn at Wildcat Mountain recipes:
Creamy Fruit Dressing, page 108
Light Chocolate Ambrosia Roll, page 195

Sour Cream-Cinnamon Breakfast Cake

Ingredients:

4 eggs
1/2 cup sugar
3/4 cup vegetable oil
1 package yellow cake mix
1 cup sour cream
3/4 cup walnuts, chopped
1/4 cup dark brown sugar
1 tablespoon cinnamon

Also:

Powdered sugar

> Beat the eggs until thick and fluffy.
> Add the sugar and oil and beat again.
> Blend in the cake mix, sour cream and nuts.
> Pour half of the batter into a well-greased bundt pan.
> Mix together the brown sugar and cinnamon and sprinkle over the batter. Swirl it in lightly with a knife.
> Pour the remaining batter on top.
> Bake in a 350-degree oven for 45 to 60 minutes. Unmold and dust with powdered sugar.

from **The Bridge Street Inn**
113 Michigan Avenue
Charlevoix, Michigan 49720
616-547-6606

"A word of caution: We may be habit-forming," says the brochure to Penny Shaw's nine guest-room inn. That applies, as well, to this coffeecake, which is served in the dining room or on the outside deck. From there, guests have a hilltop view of downtown Charlevoix, Lake Michigan, Round Lake, Lake Charlevoix and the drawbridge, under which the ferry to Beaver Island and fleets of Lake Michigan pleasure boats must travel.

This 1895 inn was the private residence of the builders of the grand Beach Hotel nearby. As the era of huge, splendid hotels ended, many hotels and guest cottages were torn down. The Bridge Street Inn is one of the few that escaped decay or development. The guest-rooms are decorated in antiques and have hardwood floors with floral rugs. Downstairs, the living room is open to guests, who can help themselves to a glass of sherry or port by the original fireplace or drink iced tea in the outdoor sitting area.

Sourdough Coffeecake and Starter

Ingredients:

1 cup sourdough
1/3 cup vegetable oil
3/4 cup sugar
1 egg
1 cup flour
3/4 teaspoon baking soda
1 teaspoon salt
1 teaspoon cinnamon

For the Starter:
1 package dry yeast
2-1/2 cups warm water
2 cups sifted flour
1 tablespoon sugar

Topping for coffeecake:
3/4 cup brown sugar
1/4 cup margarine
2 tablespoons flour
1 teaspoon cinnamon

> To make the starter, dissolve yeast in 1/2 cup of the water. Then stir in the rest of ingredients and beat until it's smooth.
> Cover with cheesecloth and let stand at room temperature for 5 to 10 days, stirring two or three times a day.
> After it has stood for at least 5 days, cover and refrigerate until used.
> After using starter, add 3/4 cup flour, 3/4 cup water and 1 teaspoon sugar to remaining starter. Let it stand at room temperature until bubbly - at least one day. Refrigerate. If not used in 10 days, add 1 teaspoon sugar. Repeat adding sugar every 10 days.
> For the coffeecake, mix the ingredients in order given.
> Pour into a greased 9 x 9-inch cake pan. Sprinkle on topping. Bake at 350 degrees for 35-40 minutes.

from **Hillside B&B**
Route 1-A, West Lakeshore Road
Cedar, Michigan 49621
616-228-6106

"Sourdough Coffeecake is almost always served at every breakfast," said Jan Kerr, whose inn is only 20 minutes away from Traverse City and 20 from the Sleeping Bear Dunes National Lakeshore. "I do not dare *not* serve it. Repeats and referrals always ask about it." Jan says the starter "may seem a nuisance, but it is wonderful to have on hand. There are so many good things to make with it."

Guests here enjoy their coffeecake in the dining room of this 1898 farmhouse, looking out over Lake Leelanau. One guest, a minister, has been quoted as saying, "The view of the lake is heavenly and the coffeecake divine." The sourdough pancakes, usually a winter treat, are out-of-this-world, too.

Another Hillside B&B recipe:
Sourdough Pancakes, page 141

Streusel Coffeecake

Ingredients:

3/4 cup milk
1/2 cup shortening
1/2 cup sugar
1 teaspoon salt
2 tablespoons dry yeast
1/2 cup lukewarm water
4 to 5 cups flour
2 eggs

Streusel Topping:
1 cup flour
1 cup sugar
1/2 to 2/3 cup soft butter

Also:

Powdered sugar frosting, optional

> Scald milk by heating it in a saucepan until a skin forms across the top.
> Add shortening, sugar and salt. Cool to lukewarm.
> Sprinkle yeast on lukewarm water. Stir to dissolve.
> Add 1-1/2 cups flour to milk mixture and beat by hand.
> Add eggs and yeast.
> Add enough flour to make a soft dough that leaves the sides of the bowl.
> Knead dough on lightly floured board until smooth and satiny.
> Place in greased bowl, set in warm place and let rise until double, about 1-1/2 hours.
> Grease five 8 or 9-inch pie pans and put a small amount of risen dough in each pan.
Spread the dough out to 1-inch thickness.
> Mix streusel topping ingredients as if mixing pie crust, until it is crumbly. Sprinkle on top of the coffeecake dough.
> Let rise 45 minutes in warm place. Bake in a 375-degree oven for 20 minutes or until nicely browned. Optional: Drizzle with powdered sugar frosting when cool.

from **Evergreen Knoll Acres**
Country Bed & Breakfast
Rural Route 1, Box 145
Lake City, Minnesota 55041
612-345-2257

"I also use this same dough for caramel rolls and frosted rolls," said Innkeeper Bev Meyer. She serves this favorite coffeecake to almost all her guests, who enjoy being part of a working dairy farm, if only for overnight. Three guest-rooms are available in this huge farmhouse.

Other Evergreen Knoll Acres recipes:
Aunt Clara's Strawberry Preserves, page 99
Strawberry Cheddar Cheesecake, page 179
Fresh Fruit Pizza, page 205

There's only one caution when it comes to making most muffins: don't "over-mix." If you do, they may be dry with tunnels inside. Otherwise, from-scratch muffins are surprisingly easy to stir up. Muffins, scones, biscuits and crumpets are great for lunches and dinners, too. Muffins, especially, have been showing up in more bakeries, restaurants and even as fast-food franchises. No wonder. They're satisfying, easy to make and versatile enough to encompass a huge variety of ingredients. Try them with the preserves and butters beginning on page 90.

Muffins, Scones
Biscuits & Crumpets

Cedarburg Apple Muffins

Ingredients:

1 cup butter
1 cup sugar
1/2 cup brown sugar
1 cup buttermilk
2 eggs
1 teaspoon baking powder
1 teaspoon baking soda
1/2 teaspoon salt
2 teaspoons cinnamon
2-1/2 cups flour
2 cups diced apples, preferably from a Cedarburg orchard

Topping:
1/2 cup pecans, chopped
1/2 cup sugar
1 teaspoon cinnamon

> Mix all ingredients together.
> Spoon into well-greased muffin tins until two-thirds full.
> Sprinkle with topping.
> Bake at 350 degrees for 15-20 minutes.

from **The Stagecoach Inn
Bed & Breakfast**
**W6I N520 Washington Avenue
Cedarburg, Wisconsin 53012
414-375-0208**

Marge Bahringer, one of the innkeepers at this 12 guest-room B&B inn, developed this recipe using local apples. Hot muffins are one of the specialties at the Stagecoach Inn, located on Cedarburg's main street. Guests are served breakfast in the gathering room downstairs or, in the summer, on a deck out in back.

The inn was built from native stone in the early 1800s and it operated as the Central House hotel at least through the 1850s. Liz and Brook Brown bought it in 1984 when it needed much work and they saw the building's potential. After much restoration, the downstairs now has a friendly gathering room for card games. Across the hall is a well-known candy shop and in the back is a small bookstore. All the guest-rooms are on the second and third floors and are decorated with antiques.

Another Stagecoach Inn B&B recipe:
Historic Apple Cake, page 31

Whole Wheat Apple Nut Oatmeal Muffins

Ingredients:

1 cup flour
3/4 cup whole wheat flour
2 teaspoons baking powder
1 teaspoon baking soda
1 cup old-fashioned rolled oats
1/2 cup raisins
1/2 cup nuts
1 cup coarsely-grated apples
1 jumbo egg
1 jumbo egg white
1 cup apple juice
2 tablespoons apple juice concentrate, thawed
3 tablespoons butter, melted

Topping:
2 tablespoons sugar
1 tablespoon brown sugar
1/2 teaspoon cinnamon
1 tablespoon butter, melted
1 cup apples, coarsely grated
1 cup crunchy granola

> In a large bowl, mix the flours, baking powder, baking soda and oatmeal.
> Add raisins, nuts and apples and mix thoroughly. Set aside.
> Beat the egg and egg white until frothy. Blend in apple juice, concentrate and butter.
> Combine egg mixture with flour mixture. Blend just until all ingredients are moist.
> Fill 12 greased muffin tins two-thirds full.
> For the topping, mix sugars and cinnamon, then set aside.
> Combine butter and apples, then quickly add granola and blend.
> Sprinkle granola mixture over the tops of the muffins, then top it with the sugar mixture.
> Bake at 400 degrees for 25-30 minutes. Cool on a wire rack.

from **The Old Holland Inn**
133 West 11th Street
Holland, Michigan 49423
616-396-6601

Innkeeper Fran Plaggemars was on a quest, said her husband, Dave, to find "the perfect healthy muffin" for Dave, who runs marathons. "As guests wandered into the kitchen, however, they were overtaken by the sight and smell of these beauties," he said. "These muffins now share equal billing with the rest of the pastries." Guests are treated to pastries, fresh fruit and cheeses for breakfast in the dining room or on the patio.

Other Old Holland Inn recipes:
Poppy Seed Orange Date-Nut Bread, page 75
Poached Pears in Cranapple Juice, page 115
Chilled Pineapple Peach Soup, page 210

Apple Bran Muffins

Ingredients:

1 cup unsweetened applesauce
1 cup milk
1 egg
1/3 cup vegetable oil
1/4 cup nuts, raisins or dates, chopped
1-1/2 cups bran cereal
1-1/4 cups flour
1 tablespoon baking powder
1/2 teaspoon salt
1/2 cup sugar

> Mix applesauce, milk, egg and oil. Add the bran cereal and let it all stand for 15 minutes.
> Beat cereal mixture well. Add dry ingredients and stir only until they are mixed in.
> Spoon the batter evenly into 12 paper-lined muffin tins.
> Bake at 400 degrees for 18 to 20 minutes.

from **Eden B&B**
Rural Route 1, Box 215
Dodge Center, Minnesota 55927
507-527-2311

These muffins are just part of a large breakfast served every morning by Innkeeper Margaret Chapin in the dining room of this 1898 farm home. If it's a chilly day, the dining room fireplace has a fire crackling and glowing.

Margaret came to this home as a bride in 1937. Her late husband was raised here, and the home has been in the Chapin family since 1907. When it was built, "Eden was a flourishing little village that boasted two stores, a blacksmith shop, stock yards, a church, a post office and a cheese factory," said Margaret. When automobiles were commonly used, area residents bypassed Eden to patronize larger towns. By 1935 it was a ghost town, she said. Today, guests can see the parsonage and remains of the cheese factory.

The Chapins farmed here for many years, and after his retirement, her husband refinished the antiques now in use. Margaret has four guest-rooms available upstairs, and the original oak woodwork remains in the staircase and moldings. Outdoors, guests can lounge in a lawn chair under maples and pines or hike on an abandoned railroad bed.

Best-Ever Buttermilk Bran Muffins

Ingredients:

2 cups bran cereal
1 cup boiling water
1-1/2 cups sugar
1/2 cup shortening
2 eggs
1 cup raisins
2 cups buttermilk
2-1/2 cups flour
2-1/2 teaspoons baking soda
1/2 teaspoon salt

> Pour boiling water over the bran cereal.
> In another bowl, cream sugar and shortening. Add eggs and beat well.
> Stir in sifted flour, soda and salt, adding alternately with buttermilk.
> Stir in raisins and bran cereal.
> Spoon into well-greased muffin tins until two-thirds full. Bake at 375 degrees for 15-20 minutes.

from **The Gallery House**
215 North Main Street
Alma, Wisconsin 54610
608-685-4975

"This mixture may be baked immediately or held in a covered container in the refrigerator for a month," said Joan Runions, who's up early to bake and cook for the 8 a.m. breakfasts. Joan and John share a big breakfast with guests from the three guest-rooms, then open their shops downstairs at 9. Joan runs the Spice Shoppe and John has his Gallery.

John's watercolors were one of the reasons the family moved here in 1974 from Chicago. The historic mercantile building is located right across the street from Lock and Dam No. 4 on the Mississippi River. Nearby Lake Pepin "just rang bells," John said about his first glimpse. A watercolor artist needs scenery, and this Mississippi bluff area has plenty of it. The dining room where guests have breakfast looks out over the river.

Another Gallery House recipe:
Skillet Frittata, page 153

Carrot Bran Muffins

Ingredients:

3 cups flour
1 teaspoon baking soda
1-1/2 tablespoons baking powder
1/2 teaspoon salt
1 tablespoon cinnamon
2 cups bran
4 eggs
1-1/2 cups vegetable oil
1-1/4 cups dark brown sugar
1/4 cup molasses
3 cups carrots, finely grated
1 cup raisins

> Sift together flour, soda, baking powder, salt and cinnamon.
> Add bran and set aside.
> Beat eggs. Add oil, sugar and molasses.
> Add carrots, flour mixture and raisins to egg mixture.
> Fill 24 paper-lined muffin tins three-quarters full. Bake at 350 for 25 minutes.

from **The Scofield House**
908 Michigan Street
Sturgeon Bay, Wisconsin 54235
414-743-7727

"This batter refrigerates nicely and can be kept for at least a week," said Bill Cecil. He and Fran, his wife, serve breakfast to guests on his mother's Austrian china "or the Noritake I bought with my crap game winnings in Japan in 1951 while serving in the U.S. Marine Corps."

Bill also suggests a way to dress up these muffins for special occasions. "We made a hit with these at Christmas time on the buffet by baking them in mini-muffin cups and then frosting them with a cream cheese and butter frosting. They suddenly are transformed into delicious little tea cakes. One guest commented that the only reason he ate so many was that he worked up an appetite while he was removing the paper cups!"

Another Scofield House recipe:
Spiced Cider Glog, page 21

Frozen Blueberry Muffins

Ingredients:

1 cup margarine, room temperature
2 cups sugar
4 eggs, slightly beaten
2 teaspoons vanilla
4 teaspoons baking powder
1/2 teaspoon salt
4 cups flour
1 cup milk
16 ounces frozen blueberries (not thawed)

Topping:
2 tablespoons sugar
1/2 teaspoon nutmeg

> Cream margarine and sugar. Add eggs and vanilla and mix thoroughly.
> Mix in baking powder, salt, flour and milk.
> Add blueberries and blend in berries, stirring by hand.
> Spoon into 18 to 20 paper-lined muffin cups until two-thirds full.
> Sprinkle with sugar-nutmeg mixture.
> Bake at 375 degrees for 25-30 minutes.

from **The Quill and Quilt**
615 West Hoffman Street
Cannon Falls, Minnesota 55009
507-263-5507

"These muffins remain moist because of the frozen blueberries," said Denise Anderson, who was given the recipe as a gift by a local resident when the B&B first opened. Denise has been serving these muffins as one of three muffin or bread varieties on the menu every morning -- as well as fruit, an entree and breakfast meat, so no one has an excuse to leave the table hungry.

Breakfast is a long and leisurely affair in the bay-windowed dining room, where classical music plays in the background. Denise and husband David Karpinski draw on their own experience and likes and dislikes during stays at some 40 B&Bs in the U.S. and abroad. They also attended several innkeeping seminars in preparation for their opening in 1987.

Other Quill and Quilt recipes:
Banana Bread, page 70
Basic Quiche Lorraine, page 123
Raspberry Champagne Punch, page 188

Blueberry Pumpkin Muffins

Ingredients:

1-2/3 cups plus 1 tablespoon flour
1 teaspoon baking soda
1/2 teaspoon baking powder
1/2 teaspoon salt
1 teaspoon cinnamon
1/2 teaspoon allspice
1 cup (8 ounces) canned pumpkin
1/4 cup evaporated milk
1/3 cup shortening
1 cup brown sugar, firmly packed
1 egg
1 cup fresh blueberries

Streusel Topping:
2 tablespoons flour
2 tablespoons sugar
1/4 teaspoon cinnamon

> Combine first six ingredients, set aside.
> In another bowl, blend pumpkin and evaporated milk.
> In a large mixing bowl, cream shortening and sugar. Add egg and beat until fluffy.
> Add flour mixture alternately with pumpkin mixture, beating well after each addition.
> Combine blueberries and flour. Gently fold berries into batter by hand.
> Fill 18 paper-lined muffin tins three-quarters full. Sprinkle with struesel topping.
> Bake at 350 degrees for 40 minutes or until toothpick inserted in center comes out clean.

from **The Northrop House**
358 East Main Street
Owatonna, Minnesota 55060
507-451-4040

The Northrup House has three guest-rooms, all named after Northrops who were winners. Cyrus Northrop won the title of second University of Minnesota president, F.S.C. Northrop was a winning author of "Meeting of East and West," and John Northrop was a Nobel Prize winner in medical research. Another Northrop, Dr. Harson A. Northrup, was the one who owned this home and, presumably, won his wife's affection, as he bought it for her birthday present.

Innkeeper Nancy Rowe promises these muffins are winners, as well. She serves them with fresh fruit and juice to guests in the dining room, which has a stained glass built-in buffet. The home, built before the turn-of-the-century, still has many of its original stained glass windows and gleaming oak woodwork. There are two grands here: a grand staircase and a grand piano, available for guests' enjoyment. Guests also can relax in front of the library fireplace.

Fresh Cherry Muffins

Ingredients:

- 1/2 cup butter, room temperature
- 1 cup sugar
- 2 large eggs
- 1 teaspoon almond extract
- 2 teaspoons baking powder
- 1/4 teaspoon salt
- 2-1/2 cups fresh tart cherries, washed and pitted (or drained frozen cherries)
- 2 cups flour
- 1/2 cup milk
- 1 to 2 tablespoons sugar
- 1/4 teaspoon nutmeg

> Beat together butter and sugar until creamy. Beat in eggs one at a time.
> Beat in extract, baking powder and salt.
> By hand, mix cherries into batter.
> Mix in half the flour, then half the milk. Repeat with other halves.
> Divide batter into 12 muffin cups which have been thoroughly greased (or use a no-stick spray). Sprinkle with sugar and nutmeg mixture.
> Bake for 25-30 minutes at 375 degrees. Let muffins cool in the pan for 15 minutes.

from **Thorp House Inn**
4135 Bluff Road
Fish Creek, Wisconsin 54212
414-868-2444

"These are a wonderful way to show off fresh Door County cherries in season," said Christine Falck-Pedersen. "Wisconsin cranberries work equally well during the fall and winter months." Since Door County cherries are available frozen, Christine and husband Sverre can serve their guests cherry muffins year 'round at their kitchen table, and their guests usually can find frozen cherries to take home, as well.

Chris and Sverre gave up careers in the Chicago area in order to renovate this turn-of-the-century B&B home and six cottages on the hill a block from downtown Fish Creek. They did nearly all the renovating and decorating before opening the four guest-rooms in August 1986.

Other Thorp House Inn recipes:
Apricot Bread, page 69
Zucchini Chocolate Bread, page 87

Coffeecake Muffins

Ingredients:

1-1/2 cups flour
1/2 cup sugar
2 teaspoons baking powder
1/2 teaspoon salt
1/4 cup margarine
1 egg, beaten
1/2 cup milk

Topping:
1/4 cup brown sugar
1/4 cup nuts, chopped
1 tablespoon flour
1 teaspoon cinnamon
1 tablespoon butter, melted

> Sift first four ingredients into a mixing bowl.
> Cut in margarine until the mixture resembles coarse crumbs.
> Mix egg with milk. Add this mixture all at once to flour mixture. Stir just until all ingredients are moistened.
> Pour half of the batter into 12 greased muffin tins until half-full.
> Sprinkle topping mixture over batter.
> Top with the rest of the batter.
> Bake the muffins at 350 degrees for about 20 minutes.

from **The Rettig House B&B**
Middle Amana, Iowa 52307
319-622-3386

These muffins are often part of breakfast served at 8 a.m. on antique china and silver at the large dining room table of Marge and Ray Rettig. The Rettigs have operated this large home in one of the seven historic Amana villages as a B&B since 1985.

The Rettig House has a long history of providing hospitality. The home was built in 1893 of bricks that were made of native clay by the local brickyard. Originally, because the Amana Colonies were operated communally, the house served as one of the community kitchens. About 40 people ate three meals a day here. In the 1930s, then-owner Lina M. Rettig turned the Rettig House into the first eating place in the Amanas. The building later served as a boarding house for teachers at the high school next door, and then as apartments.

Today, guests find five guest-rooms furnished with Amana antiques. Marge and Ray gladly provide information on what to see and do in the Amanas. The B&B is within walking distance of a bakery, cooper shop and museum.

Cranberry Muffins

Ingredients:

  1 egg
  3/4 cup milk
  1/3 cup vegetable oil
  1-3/4 cups flour
  1/2 cup sugar
  2-1/2 teaspoons baking powder
  Pinch of salt
  1 cup cranberries, chopped

> Beat egg, milk and oil in a small bowl.
> Stir together flour, baking powder and salt in a large bowl.
> Stir cranberries into the flour mixture. Make a "well" in the middle.
> Add egg mixture to the well all at once and stir just until ingredients are moistened.
> Spoon batter into 12 greased or paper-lined muffin cups.
> Bake at 400 degrees for 20-25 minutes.

from **Young's Island B&B**
Gunflint Trail 67-1
Grand Marais, Minnesota 55604
1-800-322-8327

Breakfast always tastes great at Barbara and Ted Young's log cabin B&B, in part because it's good cookin' and in part because it took a little extra effort to get there. Guests drive 32 miles up the Gunflint Trail, a blacktop road that cuts inland from Grand Marias through moose and wolf country. Then, at Poplar Lake, Barb or Ted meet guests and they either canoe, motorboat, cross-country ski, or dog sled over to the island.

Youngs moved to the family cabin bordering the Boundary Waters Canoe Area in 1974. Their son, Joey, may be coaxed into giving guests an island tour or instructions in cross-country skiing. Youngs run a popular winter x-c ski business in which skiers stay overnight on the ski trail in a heated Mongolian yurt, and Ted gives dog sled rides and mushing classes. At the B&B, winter guests can enjoy a sauna and summer guests can swim, fish and canoe right out in front of the cabin.

Another Young's Island recipe:
Baked Eggs, page 118

Laurie's Poppy Seed Muffins

Ingredients:

 2-1/2 cups sugar
 2 cups evaporated milk
 5 eggs
 1/2 cup milk
 5 cups flour
 4-1/2 teaspoons baking powder
 1/2 teaspoon salt
 1/2 cup poppy seeds
 1-1/2 teaspoons vanilla

> Combine sugar, evaporated milk, eggs and milk in a bowl.
> In another bowl, sift together flour, baking powder and salt.
> Add milk and egg mixture to dry ingredients.
> Mix in poppy seeds and vanilla. Beat until smooth.
> Pour into 40 greased miniature muffin tins until they are three-quarters full.
> Bake at 350 degrees for 25-35 minutes.

from **Thorwood**
Fourth and Pine
Hastings, Minnesota 55033
612-437-3297

Innkeeper Pam Thorsen finally got this recipe from her sister Laurie, who'd been bringing these muffins to family gatherings for years. "It took two years of begging to get it from her," Pam said. Warm muffins are just part of a huge Thorwood breakfast that is either served in the dining room or in breakfast baskets delivered to the doors of eight romantic guest-rooms.

Pam and Dick Thorsen bought this building, a former mansion, hospital and apartment house, in 1979 and it became one of Minnesota's first B&Bs when it opened with two rooms in February 1983. Today, Thorwood is one of the state's most popular inns and is only a half-hour drive from the Twin Cities. In between came years of restoration and redecorating work, plus being very involved in the B&B movement -- Pam is one of the founders of the Minnesota Historic B&B Association.

Another Thorwood recipe:
Candied Violets, page 172

Cherie's Spicy Pumpkin Muffins

Ingredients:

    3-1/2 cups flour
    1/2 teaspoon salt
    2 teaspoons baking soda
    2 teaspoons pumpkin pie spice
    1 teaspoon nutmeg
    3 cups sugar
    1 cup vegetable oil
    1 cup water
    2 cups pumpkin
    4 eggs
    1/2 cup nuts, chopped

> Sift together dry ingredients in large bowl. Stir in nuts.
> In another bowl, add beaten eggs to sugar, oil, water and pumpkin.
> Blend egg mixture into dry ingredients.
> Fill approximately 24 greased or paper-lined muffin cups three-quarters full.
> Bake at 400 degrees for about 15-20 minutes.

from **The White Lace Inn**
16 North Fifth Avenue
Sturgeon Bay, Wisconsin 54235
414-743-1105

This recipe also can be made in two loaf pans and baked for about an hour at
350 degrees, said Bonnie Statz, who, with husband Dennis, operate this
1903 Victorian inn. Actually, they have three historic homes, which adjoin
at the gardens in the back, for a total of 15 romantic guest-rooms.

Dennis and Bonnie opened Sturgeon Bay's first B&B inn in 1982. They
bought the 1903 home in April 1982 and had it restored and the first five
rooms open by that July. An 1880s farm-style home was moved to their
one-acre lot a year later and restored, adding six guest-rooms. Recently,
an adjacent house was purchased and restored, with four more rooms.

Guests at all the houses gather for breakfast in the dining room of the main
house from 8 to 10 each morning. This recipe was perfected by Cherie
Therrien, an assistant innkeeper at the White Lace Inn.

Other White Lace Inn recipes:
Scandinavian Fruit Soup, page 116
Zingy Cheese and Egg Casserole, page 127

Red Raspberry Muffins

Ingredients:

1/4 cup shortening
1/2 cup sugar
2 eggs, beaten
2 cups flour
4 teaspoons baking powder
1 teaspoon salt
2/3 cup milk
1-1/2 cups fresh raspberries (or well-drained frozen berries)

> Cream shortening and add sugar gradually. Add eggs.
> Mix dry ingredients. Add alternately with milk to egg mixture.
> Wash the berries. Stir gently into the batter.
> Fill 18 greased muffin cups half to two-thirds full.
> Bake at 400 degrees for about 20 minutes.

from **Foxmoor B&B**
P.O. Box 194
Wilmot, Wisconsin 53192
414-862-6161

Innkeeper Marylyn Mayer says strawberries can be substituted if they are cut into "at least four pieces per berry." Summer and fall guests at her farm B&B, however, rarely have to go without raspberries. "Guests can pick their own from our huge garden while cows watch," she said.

Guests at this three guest-room B&B often are invited to join in the day's activity, be it bread baking, jelly making, canning, refinishing furniture or creating stained glass. Marylyn, a former teacher and corporate manager, enjoys having guests who are interested in country life. She and husband Fred have 100 acres and a garden of almost an acre, too prolific for their use alone. Guests are told to make themselves at home, and that may include going home with extra rhubarb or a pumpkin. The charcoal grill and picnic table outside are available for guests' use, as is the refrigerator, fireplace and VCR in the living room.

Guests can arranged to be picked up at this B&B for canoe trips on three area waterways. Swimming, fishing, boating, horseback riding, hunting, cross-country and downhill skiing all are within five miles of Foxmoor.

Strawberry-Rhubarb Muffins

Ingredients:

    1-3/4 cups flour
    1/2 cup sugar
    2-1/2 teaspoons baking powder
    3/4 teaspoon salt
    1 egg, slightly beaten
    3/4 cup milk
    1/3 cup vegetable oil
    3/4 cup fresh rhubarb, minced
    1/2 cup fresh strawberries, sliced

Also:

    6 small strawberries, halved
    Sugar for sprinkling

> Mix dry ingredients in a large bowl.

> In a small bowl, combine egg, milk and oil. Stir the liquids into the flour mixture with a fork just until moistened.

> Fold rhubarb and sliced strawberries into the batter.

> Fill 12 greased muffin tins three-quarters full. Press a strawberry half gently into the top of each muffin. Sprinkle tops with sugar.

> Bake at 400 degrees for 20-25 minutes.

from **The Renaissance Inn**
414 Maple Drive
Sister Bay, Wisconsin 54234
414-854-5107

Innkeeper JoDee Faller has these muffins whipped up, popped in the oven and ready to eat by 9 a.m. each day, when breakfast is served downstairs in the cozy restaurant. This inn has five guest-rooms upstairs, and John and JoDee have a small, gourmet seafood restaurant downstairs. The restaurant is open only for lunch in the summer and for dinners year 'round, so guests have the place to themselves for breakfast.

JoDee opened the B&B in July 1983 soon after buying the historic building and moving to Door County. Quilts on the beds were handmade by JoDee's mother and sister. One upstairs room is used by guests as a parlor for board games and TV, and guests have a separate entrance.

Other Renaissance Inn recipes:
Zucchini Frittata, page 154
Zucchini Patties, page 173

Surprise Muffins

Ingredients:

1 egg
1/2 cup milk
1/4 cup vegetable oil
1-1/2 cups flour
2 teaspoons baking powder
1/2 cup sugar
1/2 teaspoon salt
Your favorite preserves

> In a large bowl, beat the egg. Stir in milk and oil.
> Mix in all other ingredients except preserves. Stir just until flour is moistened. The batter should be lumpy.
> Fill 12 greased muffin cups only half-full.
> Drop 1 teaspoon preserves in the center of each. Add batter to fill the cup two-thirds full.
> Bake at 350 degrees for 20-25 minutes.

from **The Inn at Cedar Crossing**
336 Louisiana Street
Sturgeon Bay, Wisconsin 54235
414-743-4200

When you bite into one of these muffins, you'll see what the surprise is. If the preserves you used were cherry jams brought home from Door County, you've just gotten cherry pie for breakfast. These muffins need no butter and are very good served hot or cold.

At the Inn at Cedar Crossing, Terry Wulf's guests are treated to a hearty continental breakfast, possibly including these muffins. Guests may have breakfast from 8-10 a.m. in the dining room downstairs, which also serves as a restaurant open for breakfast, lunch and dinner. The inn's nine guest-rooms are located on the second floor of this historic mercantile building.

Other Inn at Cedar Crossing recipes:
Apple Yogurt Coffeecake, page 30
Fresh Rhubarb Bread, page 84
Zucchini Chocolate Nut Bread, page 88
Nectarines with Cream Anglaise, page 113
Hot Apple Crisp, page 192
Crispy Caramel Corn, page 202

Sweet Potato Muffins

Ingredients:

1-1/2 cups flour
2 teaspoons baking powder
1/2 teaspoon cinnamon
1/8 teaspoon nutmeg
1/8 teaspoon salt
2/3 cup sugar
2/3 cup sweet potato, peeled, cooked and mashed
1/2 cup milk
1/4 cup butter, melted
1 large egg
1/2 cup raisins, chopped

Topping:
2 tablespoons sugar
1/4 teaspoon cinnamon

> Sift together first five ingredients.
> In a large bowl, beat sugar, sweet potato, milk, butter and egg with a wire whisk until well mixed.
> Add dry ingredients and stir just until moistened. Fold in raisins.
> If using seasoned cast iron muffin molds, place them in the 400-degree oven to heat. When hot, grease the molds.
> Fill 16 molds or greased muffin tins with the batter. Add topping. Bake at 400 degrees for about 15 minutes or until top springs back when lightly touched.

from **The Westerfield House**
Rural Route 2, Box 34
Freeburg, Illinois 62243
618-539-5643

Marilyn Westerfield makes these muffins in heart-shaped molds for guests staying in the log cabin B&B she and husband Jim operate. The cast iron molds are just one reflection of colonial America that the Westerfields have incorporated here. Jim and Marilyn opened their B&B in 1982. In a year, they expanded to include gourmet dinners, and have since been featured in several cooking magazines and books. They offer guests almost complete immersion into the past through attention to details, with period dress, antique collections ranging from 200-year-old Windsor chairs to porcelain dolls, and an old-fashioned herb garden with 30 species of mint.

Another Westerfield House recipe:
Chokahlua Cheesecake, page 176

Zucchini Pineapple Muffins

Ingredients:

3 eggs
1 cup vegetable oil
2 cups sugar
2 teaspoons vanilla
2 cups unpeeled zucchini, shredded
1 small can (8-1/4 ounces) crushed or tidbit pineapple, drained
3 cups flour
2 teaspoons baking soda
1-1/2 teaspoon cinnamon
1 teaspoon salt
3/4 teaspoon nutmeg
1/4 teaspoon baking powder
1 cup dates or raisins, chopped
1 cup nuts, chopped

> Beat eggs, oil, sugar and vanilla until thick.
> Stir in remaining ingredients. Mix well.
> Fill 24 greased or paper-lined muffin tins two-thirds full with batter.
> Bake at 350 degrees for 25-30 minutes or until a toothpick inserted in the middle comes out clean.

from **Noni's B&B**
516 West Main Street
Warren, Illinois 61087
815-745-2045

Guests at Naomi McCool's B&B are served these muffins warm from the oven either in the sunroom or the dining room of her 150-year-old home. "Noni" opened the B&B in 1987 after being inspired by Kathleen Webster, who works with many B&B operators in her position as director of the county Convention and Visitors' Bureau. Warren is in the same county and only 30 miles from Galena, an historic town in northwestern Illinois that has become a very popular destination in the last few years. Along with popularity came more than two dozen B&Bs in the area, many in beautifully-restored historic homes.

Noni said she has enjoyed having visitors come share her nine-room home with two guest-rooms. She works full-time as a bookkeeper and can't do the traveling herself, so she loves to have the world come to her.

Another Noni's B&B recipe:
Irish Soda Bread, page 184

Dried Cherry Scones

Ingredients:

- 2 cups flour
- 4 teaspoons baking powder
- 1/2 teaspoon salt
- 1/4 cup butter
- 3 tablespoons sugar
- 1/2 cup dried tart Michigan cherries
- 1/2 to 3/4 cups milk

> Sift flour, salt and baking powder in a bowl. Cut in butter with a pastry blender until mixture resembles gravel.
> Add sugar and cherries.
> Mix in enough milk to make a soft -- but not wet -- dough.
> On a floured surface, roll or pat out to 1/2 to 3/4-inch thick. Cut into 2-inch rounds.
> Place on a pre-heated cookie sheet and bake near the top of a 450-degree oven for 10-12 minutes. "Best served fresh."

Makes 13 scones, a baker's dozen

from **The Urban Retreat**
2759 Canterbury Road
Ann Arbor, Michigan 48104
313-971-8110

"Dried Michigan cherries are a wonderful alternative to raisins or currants. They can be plumped before adding them to a recipe or used as is," said Gloria Krys, who loves to feature Michigan fruit at the B&B she and André Rosalik operate 10 minutes from downtown Ann Arbor and the U of M. "We find them in bulk food or health food stores or they can be ordered from American Spoon Foods in Petoskey, Michigan."
(In Michigan, call 1-800-237-7984; elsewhere, 1-800-222-5886. American Spoon Foods also sells dried morels, blueberries and cranberries, plus jams and other fruit products.)

Gloria calls these scones "foolproof and a wonderful addition to the breakfast table. We like serving these with Devonshire cream or unsalted butter."

Other Urban Retreat recipes:
Blueberry Jam, page 93
Peach-Orange Marmalade, page 95

Casey's Cream Scones

Ingredients:

- 1/2 cup raisins
- Orange-flavored liqueur
- 2 cups flour
- 2 teaspoons baking powder
- 1 tablespoon sugar
- 1/4 teaspoon salt
- 6 tablespoons butter, cut into several pieces
- 2 eggs, beaten
- 1/2 cup heavy cream

> Ahead of time, soak the raisins in liqueur.
> Combine dry ingredients. Cut in the butter with a pastry blender until it resembles coarse meal.
> Drain the liqueur from the raisins. Mix the eggs, cream and raisins.
> Add the egg mixture to the flour mixture. Stir just until "pulled together."
> Turn the dough out on a floured board. Knead for one minute.
> Pat the dough into a round, about 3/4-inch thick. Cut into eight wedges.
> Place on a lightly-greased baking sheet. Bake at 425 degrees for about 15 minutes, until golden.

Makes 8 scones

from **Linné Bed & Breakfast**
2645 Fremont Avenue South
Minneapolis, Minnesota 55408
612-377-4418

This recipe, said Innkeeper Robert Torsten Eriksson, was accidental -- "adding more heavy cream than was called for and soaking the raisins in Triple Sec rather than brandy. The result was not a disappointment but a triumph! These are served warm from the oven, tucked in a linen-lined basket and with three or four jams and marmalades."

There's nothing accidental about the B&B he and wife Casey Higgins opened in 1987. Casey, a nurse and chef, wanted to put her chef skills to part-time work, and found the B&B an ideal supplement to nursing. She and Robert, also a nurse, named their 1896 home after a favorite Swedish flower.

Other Linné recipes:
Eggs Linné, page 120
Plättar (Swedish Pancakes), page 138

Nutty Scones

Ingredients:
2 tablespoons lightly salted butter
2 tablespoons shortening
1/3 cup sugar
1 egg
1-1/8 cups milk
2 teaspoons baking powder
4-1/2 cups cake flour
1/2 cup raisins or other dried fruit
1/2 cup walnuts or pecans

Strawberry Butter:
1 cup butter, softened
1/4 cup strawberries, puréed

Also:
Egg wash of egg yolk and water
Cinnamon-sugar mixture

> Cream sugar, butter and shortening.
> Add the egg. Mix and scrape the bowl well.
> Add sifted flour, baking powder and milk. Do not over-mix.
> Mix in raisins and nuts only until incorporated. Refrigerate one hour before using.
> Roll the dough out to 1/2-inch thick and cut into heart shapes with a cookie cutter. Place on a greased cookie sheet.
> Brush with an egg wash and sprinkle with coarse sugar or cinnamon sugar.
> Bake at 350 degrees only until scones are golden brown. Serve with Strawberry Butter.

Makes 36 scones

from **The Montague Inn**
1581 South Washington Avenue
Saginaw, Michigan 48601
517-752-3939

Guests who are staying in this restored mansion of a sugar beet magnate may find these scones in their morning breadbasket. Innkeeper Norm Kinney is particularly fond of the English tradition of scones, and he was glad to offer afternoon teas, where scones are found along with assorted pastries. The Montague Inn's high teas are in addition to by-reservation-only gourmet luncheons and dinners.

This luxurious establishment, built in 1929, has 13 bedrooms in the main house from which guests can choose, plus five more in the guest house. The Georgian mansion, restored top to bottom, is situated on eight acres in a neighborhood of fine historic homes.

Applesauce Biscuits

Ingredients:

2 cups flour
3 teaspoons baking powder
1/4 teaspoon baking soda
1 teaspoon salt
3 tablespoons shortening
1 egg, beaten
1/2 cup unsweetened applesauce
1/4 cup sour cream
1/2 cup cheddar cheese, grated

> Sift together the first four ingredients. Cut in shortening.
> Combine the rest of the ingredients and add to the dry ingredients. Mix quickly.
> Turn out on a floured surface and knead for only a few seconds.
> Roll out to 1/2-inch thick. Cut with 2-inch biscuit circles.
> Place on an ungreased baking sheet. Sprinkle with cheese.
> Bake at 400 degrees for 15 minutes.

Makes 12 biscuits

from **The Parkside**
402 East North Street
Appleton, Wisconsin 54911
414-733-0200

"My Midwestern roots definitely show up in my favorite recipes," said Innkeeper Bonnie Riley, who devised this recipe while teaching a bread baking workshop. "I tend to like my morning breads fairly simple to allow for plenty of whipped Wisconsin butter and the summer's fruit preserves!"

The Parkside's guests, who rent the entire third floor apartment, may be treated to these biscuits as part of the breakfast Bonnie serves downstairs in the dining room or to the guest suite on a breakfast tray at a time arranged the night before. Fresh fruit is waiting in the suite when guests arrive. They can help themselves to coffee downstairs any time, since the coffee pot is always on, or they can use the kitchen in the suite to brew their own. The kitchen has such essentials as coffee, soda pop and wine.

Other Parkside recipes:
Baking Powder Biscuits, page 66
Wassail, page 190

Cinnamon Raisin Biscuits

Ingredients:

2 cups flour
1/3 cup shortening
1 teaspooon cinnamon-sugar
1/2 teaspoon salt
1 teaspoon baking powder
1/2 cup raisins
2/3 to 3/4 cup milk

Also:

Powdered sugar glaze, optional

> Sift flour. Mix all ingredients and fold in cinnamon-sugar (about 1/3 teaspoon cinnamon, 2/3 teaspoon sugar).
> On a floured surface, roll out to 1/2 to 3/4-inch thick.
> Using a round biscuit cutter, cut in circles.
> Place on a greased cookie sheet. Bake at 450 degrees for 10 to 12 minutes.
> Optional: Drizzle with a powdered sugar glaze made by mixing powdered sugar with a little milk or cream.

from **The Scanlan House**
708 Parkway South
Lanesboro, Minnesota 55949
507-467-2158

"These biscuits are really a light touch to top off breakfast," said Mary Mensing. "They are light and flaky with a sweet roll satisfaction for anyone with the sweet tooth urge."

Mary, husband Gene and daughter Kirsten all are involved in the kitchen creations at this Victorian B&B, located in a Root River town in southeastern Minnesota. The home was built in 1889 by Mikael Scanlan, whose family helped settle Lanesboro and was involved in banking and jewelry businesses.

Mensings moved to Lanesboro in 1987 from Galesville, Wis., in order to open the B&B in this home, listed on the National Register of Historic Places. Five rooms are available as guest-rooms, furnished in antiques. The home still has much of its original woodwork and leaded glass windows. Summer guests may enjoy breakfast on the patio.

Another Scanlan House recipe:
Tomato Bites, page 213

Baking Powder Biscuits

Ingredients:

2 cups flour
2 tablespoons baking powder
1-1/2 teaspoons salt
3/4 cup milk
3 tablespoons sugar
1/3 cup butter or margarine
Raisins, optional

Glaze:
1 cup powdered sugar
1 tablespoon cream
Fresh Blueberry Sauce:
2-1/2 cups fresh blueberries
3 tablespoons cornstarch
1-1/4 cups sugar
1/2 cup water

> Sift the dry ingredients together three times.
> Cut in the butter.
> Add milk and mix with a spoon. Add raisins, if desired.
> Turn out on a floured surface and knead for only a few seconds.
> Roll out to 1/2-inch thick. Cut with 2-inch biscuit circles.
> Place on an ungreased baking sheet. Bake at 400 degrees for 20 minutes.
> For a glaze, mix powdered sugar and cream. Drizzle over warm biscuits.
> For Fresh Blueberry Sauce, cook 1-1/2 cups blueberries and the rest of ingredients in a saucepan over medium-high heat until thick. Remove from heat and cool.
> Stir in the remaining 1 cup blueberries. Chill before serving over biscuits.

Makes 12 biscuits

from **The Parkside**
402 East North Street
Appleton, Wisconsin 54911
414-733-0200

These biscuits turn out "light, high and fluffly moist, with or without raisins, with or without glaze," said Bonnie Riley, who believes the bigger these biscuits are, the better. They are even better with blueberry sauce.

Bonnie became an innkeeper when she opened the Parkside in 1985, a year after she and her family moved to Appleton. As a teen, she had spent her summers working in Lake Geneva, Wis., in the tourism business, so she was confident she'd like innkeeping. She looked for a home in Appleton with B&B potential. The home is across the street from a park and just two blocks from Lawrence University. Converting the third floor apartment to a B&B suite made perfect sense, and guests can see the park from the suite.

Other Parkside recipes:
Applesauce Biscuits, page 64
Wassail, page 190

Duke House Crumpets (English Muffins)

Ingredients:

1 small potato, peeled and quartered
2 packages dry yeast
1 teaspoon sugar
1 teaspoon salt
2-1/2 cups flour, sifted
Softened butter

> Boil the potato in 1-1/2 cups salted water for 15 minutes or until very soft.
> Remove the potato, mash it and set aside. Reserve the potato water.
> In a half-cup of the warm potato water, dissolve the yeast and sugar. Let stand 10 minutes or until bubbly.
> Add remaining potato water and salt. Work in mashed potato and enough flour to make a heavy batter.
> Cover and let rise for 30 minutes in a warm place.
> With a wooden spoon, beat rapidly for five minutes. Cover. Let rise again for 30 minutes.
> Repeat beating and rising twice more at half-hour intervals.
> Grease the inside of four muffin rings (or well-washed tuna cans with both ends removed).
> Heat a griddle and keep at low, even heat. Grease it lightly with butter.
> Place muffin rings around the sides of the griddle. Fill half-full with batter.
> "Bake" for about 15 minutes. Batter will rise as it bakes. Turn and bake for 5 minutes.
> Remove from heat and remove rings. Re-grease the rings and refill until 12 are made.
> At serving time, spread the rough side (with the holes) generously with butter. Toast under a broiler. Serve with preserves.

from **The Duke House**
618 Maiden Street
Mineral Point, Wisconsin 53565
608-987-2821

Since Mineral Point, settled by Cornish miners, is fond of its British heritage, and since Darlene and Tom Duke run "a traditional English-style B&B," these crumpets are sometimes on the breakfast table "so our guests may experience a little bit of England while still in America," said Darlene.

The Dukes also encourage guests to have a pasty and figgyhobbin and see the restored Cornish homes while visiting town. Then guests retire to one of three Colonial-style guest-rooms in this historic home, which Tom and Darlene purchased and opened in 1983. Guests are treated to an evening social hour, and at breakfast, goldfinches often come to the window to feed.

Any bread, unless it's burned to a crisp, can be edible if you put enough butter on top. But these breads are so moist and flavorful that they need no butter at all. Some can be whipped up in just a few minutes. Others have yeast and require time to "rise." But any way you slice it, there's nothing like the smell of bread baking, or the taste of hot rolls right from the oven. It's no surprise that in the past decade or so, cooks seemed to have come back to homemade bread, for health as well as cost and taste reasons. Enjoy the wide variety of breads, buns, rolls, doughnuts and poundcakes in this chapter.

Breads

Apricot Bread

Ingredients:

- 1 cup dried apricots
- 1/2 cup hot water
- 1 cup sugar
- 1 cup brown sugar
- 3 cups flour
- 1/2 teaspoon baking soda
- 2 teaspoons baking powder
- 1/2 teaspoon salt
- 3 eggs, beaten
- 1 cup sour cream
- 1 cup pecans, chopped

> Chop apricots into small pieces and put into the hot water to soak.
> Sift dry ingredients together. Add eggs.
> Stir in sour cream and pecans.
> Add soaked apricots, undrained.
> Divide between two greased loaf pans.
> Bake for 45 minutes-1 hour at 350 degrees.

from **Thorp House Inn**
4135 Bluff Road
Fish Creek, Wisconsin 54212
414-868-2444

Guests at this four guest-room B&B may wander downstairs to the kitchen anytime between 8 and 10 for a continental breakfast including homebaked breads and muffins such as this. Christine and/or Sverre Falck-Pedersen are on hand to serve and share recommendations for a day in Door County.

Nearly every visitor takes in Peninsula State Park, four blocks from this hillside B&B. This large park has a bike trail, hiking trails, a golf course, an observation tower and plenty of Lake Michigan beaches, several of which are sought out for sunset viewing. Guests who've caught the sunset, feasted at a fish boil or enjoyed summer stock theater can return to relax on the summer porch or in front of the fireplace before heading upstairs to bed.

Other Thorp House Inn recipes:
Fresh Cherry Muffins, page 51
Zucchini Chocolate Bread, page 87

Banana Bread

Ingredients:

1/2 cup butter
1 cup sugar
2 eggs, separated
8 tablespoons cold water
3 very ripe bananas, mashed
1 teaspoon baking soda
1 teaspoon baking powder
2-1/2 cups flour

> Cream butter and sugar.
> Add egg yolks and the rest of the ingredients and mix well.
> Add the two egg whites and mix.
> Fill two greased loaf pans or four standard-sized vegetable cans two-thirds full.
> Bake at 350 degrees for one hour or until a toothpick inserted in the center comes out clean.

from **The Quill and Quilt**
615 West Hoffman Street
Cannon Falls, Minnesota 55009
507-263-5507

"This was my grandmother's recipe and it gets rave reviews from our guests," said Innkeeper Denise Anderson. Denise's family heritage shows up in more than just the banana bread. Treasured family recipes are part of the Quill and Quilt's breakfast, dinner and social hour menus. Quilts made by Denise's great-grandmother decorate the halls and bedrooms, and Denise's own handmade quilts are in each of the four guest-rooms.

Special, color-coordinated quilts were just one of the items on the agenda before opening this B&B in 1987. The 1897 home belonged to a prominent physician, and his oak and hemlock woodwork was meticulously restored. Plumbing, decorating and antiquing also were necessary in the busy three months preceeding opening.

Other Quill and Quilt recipes:
Frozen Blueberry Muffins, page 49
Basic Quiche Lorraine, page 123
Raspberry Champagne Punch, page 188

Granola Banana Bread

Ingredients:

3/4 cup brown sugar
3 tablespoons vegetable oil
2 eggs
1-1/2 cups banana, mashed
2 cups granola
2 cups whole wheat flour
1 cup stone-ground flour
1-1/2 cups milk
3-1/2 teaspoons baking powder
1/2 teaspoon salt or less

> Process all dry ingredients, except granola, in the food processor. Pour out of the food processor and set aside.
> Add all liquid ingredients, including bananas, to food processor and blend.
> Stir in granola. Let stand five minutes.
> Add dry ingredients. "Pulse" until all traces of flour have disappeared.
> Scrape down bowl and "pulse" two or three times. Let sit another five minutes.
> Bake in two medium greased loaf pans at 350 degrees for about one hour (test with knife blade in the center, and if it comes out clean, the bread is done).

from **Maggie's B&B**
2102 North Keebler Road
Collinsville, Illinois 62234
618-344-8283

"This is especially good with cream cheese or homemade jelly or preserves," said Maggie Leyda, who includes her homemade granola in this recipe. Breakfast at this B&B includes all-natural foods, and she gets her stone-ground flour from a mill in Gainesville, Missouri.

Maggie bought this former mine superintendent's house, about a half hour drive from St. Louis, after retiring in 1986. Retiring early at 62, she was bored and depressed with time on her hands, so she sold her condo and bought this old home to be a B&B. The four guest-rooms are different colors, some with heavy Victorian drapes and spreads and antique lamps.

Another Maggie's B&B recipe:
Cooked Multi-Grain Cereal, page 149

Easy A.M. Cinnamon Rolls

Ingredients:

3/4 cup sugar
1 tablespoon cinnamon
1 package dry yeast
1/4 cup warm water
4 cups flour
1 teaspoon salt
1 teaspoon lemon peel, grated
1 cup margarine
2 eggs, lightly beaten
1 cup milk, scalded
Softened butter

Icing:
Powdered sugar
Milk

> Dissolve yeast in warm water, set aside.
> In a large bowl, mix flour, salt, lemon and remaining sugar. Cut in margarine with a fork.
> In another bowl, mix eggs, cooled-down milk and yeast.
> Add to flour mixture and mix well.
> Cover tightly and refrigerate overnight.
> Mix 1/2 cup sugar and cinnamon and set aside until morning.
> In the morning, knead dough in a small amount of flour. Divide it in half.
> Roll half of the dough out on a floured board to an 18 x 18-inch square.
> Lightly spread soft butter on the rolled dough and sprinkle with sugar-cinnamon mixture.
> Roll up the dough tightly and cut in 1-inch slices. Repeat with other half of dough.
> Place far enough apart on a greased cookie sheet so they do not touch. Let them stand for 15 minutes.
> Bake for 15 minutes at 350 degrees. When cool, drizzle with milk-powdered sugar icing.

Makes 36 rolls

from **A Country Place**
Route 5, Box 43
North Shore Drive
South Haven, Michigan 49090
616-637-5523

"Ice only those rolls to be served and freeze the remainder for later use,"
said Lee Niffenegger, who may serve these rolls fresh from the oven on
china from a half dozen or so collections. "We love to set a beautiful table,
but we never get carried away with too much formality."

Other A Country Place recipes:
Blueberry Streusel Coffeecake, page 33
Hot Cooked Apples, page 104

Celia's English Coconut Tea Loaf

Ingredients:
- 1 egg
- 1-1/2 cups milk
- 1/2 teaspoon vanilla
- 1/4 teaspoon almond extract
- 1 cup shredded coconut
- 3 cups flour
- 3 teaspoons baking powder
- 1/2 teaspoon salt
- 1 cup sugar

> Combine first five ingredients in a blender. Cover and blend for 30 seconds.
> In a bowl, sift dry ingredients together. Pour blended mixture over the dry ingredients. Stir only to combine.
> Pour the batter into a greased 9 x 5-inch pan.
> Bake at 350 degrees for 70 minutes. Chill before serving.

from **The Hutchinson House**
305 Northwest Second Street
Faribault, Minnesota 55021
507-332-7519

Innkeeper Marilyn Coughlin received this recipe 20-some years ago from a British friend. "The beauty of this recipe is that it contains no additional oil other than that inherent in the coconut," Marilyn said. "It's wonderful toasted, and it is better without any additions such as jams or jellies."

Tea time in this 1892 Queen Anne mansion, built by one of the town's most successful businessmen, might be held in the formal parlor, on the wrap-around porch or by the fireplace. Marilyn's homemade breakfast is served in the front parlor. Everywhere there is natural woodwork and fine craftsmanship; John Hutchinson, a furniture maker himself, surely would approve of the home's restoration.

Marilyn opened the B&B in 1987 after months of work. One of the projects was a 19.5-foot mural of cherubs on a wall in a suite. Marilyn was an art teacher. "I cook the way I paint," she says, "creatively and originally and many times spontaneously. I always feel free to depart from the recipe."

Other Hutchinson House recipes:
Baked Stuffed Peaches, page 166
Grandma's Custard Bread Pudding, page 197

Date-Nut Bread

Ingredients:

1 cup dates, chopped
2 cups boiling water
2 teaspoons baking soda
4 cups flour
1 teaspoon salt
2 tablespoons butter
2 cups sugar
2 eggs
2 teaspoons vanilla
1 cup nuts

> Combine dates, boiling water and baking soda ("Look out! This combination sometimes boils over!"). Cool.
> Sift flour and salt.
> In another bowl, cream butter and sugar well. Add eggs, one at a time, and beat well.
> Add flour and salt alternately with the date mixture, and beat until smooth.
> Stir in the vanilla and nuts.
> Grease the sides and bottom of four #2 cans (fruit or vegetable cans washed thoroughly and with labels removed). Fill two-thirds full.
> Bake at 350 degrees for about one hour.

from **The Belle Aire Mansion**
11410 Route 20 West
Galena, Illinois 61036
815-777-0893

"This recipe has been in my family for as long as I can remember," said Innkeeper Lorraine Svec, who often serves it with breakfast entrees. The Belle Aire Mansion, however, has not been a family treasure nearly as long. She and her sister and their families began running the four guest-room B&B in the fall of 1987. They've found their work and guests fascinating.

Galena attracts many visitors to its historically-renovated downtown and hilly surroundings. This mansion is an 1836 Federal-style home on 16 acres, two miles from Galena. Travelers coming into town from Dubuque or the north will notice this estate-like place with a long driveway, barn, windmill and trees and flowers. After spending the day in downtown Galena, shopping antique stores or completing a long historic walking tour, guests return to the quiet of the country porch or living room to talk, play the piano, read or watch TV. This bread might be served as an afternoon snack.

Poppy Seed Orange Date-Nut Bread

Ingredients:

- 1 cup warm orange juice
- 1-1/2 cups warm water
- 1 package dry yeast
- 6 tablespoons honey
- 2 cups whole wheat flour
- 2 tablespoons vegetable oil
- 3 heaping tablespoons poppy seeds
- 3 tablespoons rolled oats, optional
- Juice of 1 orange
- 1 tablespoon orange rind, grated
- 1/2 cup dates, chopped
- 3/4 cup nuts, chopped
- 3-1/2 to 4 cups whole wheat flour

> Mix orange juice, water, yeast, honey and two cups flour. Let this sit until bubbly, about 30 minutes.

> Mix in the remaining ingredients, except the 3-1/2 to 4 cups flour, and knead well. Add the flour as needed to make a soft, spongy dough.

> Let the dough rise in a covered, oiled bowl until double in size, about 30 minutes.

> Put in two oiled, floured loaf pans and let rise again.

> Bake at 400 degrees for about 35 minutes.

from **The Old Holland Inn**
133 West 11th Street
Holland, Michigan 49423
616-396-6601

Fran Plaggemars has innkeeping in her blood, and this recipe proves it. Fran's grandmother ran a boarding house in Philadelphia until her 80th birthday, and this recipe was hers, though Fran has modified it a bit.

Fran knew innkeeping was for her when she and husband Dave walked into this 1895 home. It was built by the son of Holland's first mayor and owner of a leather company, Holland's major business. John Cappon built it when he was on the company's board. The home has hardwood floors and sliding oak doors built by first-generation Dutch woodworkers. Original brass lighting fixtures, fireplace and 16-inch fieldstone foundation also remain.

Other Old Holland Inn recipes:
Whole Wheat Apple Nut Oatmeal Muffins, page 45
Poached Pears in Cranapple Juice, page 115
Chilled Pineapple Peach Soup, page 210

English Muffin Loaf

<u>Ingredients:</u>

    6 cups flour, divided
    2 packages dry yeast
    1 tablespoon sugar
    1/4 teaspoon baking soda
    1-1/2 teaspoons salt
    1/2 cup water
    2 cups milk

<u>Also:</u>

    Cornmeal

> Combine half the flour, yeast, sugar, salt and soda.
> Heat milk and water until very warm. Add to the above dry ingredients.
> With a mixer, mix on low speed for two to three minutes.
> Stir in the rest of the flour to make a soft dough.
> Knead the dough on a floured board for two minutes.
> Place the dough in a greased loaf pan that has been sprinkled with cornmeal. Cover and set in a warm place to rise until doubled.
> Bake at 400 degrees for 25 minutes.

from **Silver Creek B&B**
4361 U.S. Highway 23 South
Black River, Michigan 48721
517-471-2198

"This bread makes great toast or French toast," said Innkeeper Kim Moses. She was given the recipe years ago by her great aunt. She often bakes this bread in an 1870 double-round bread pan.

Kim has lots of things from years ago at this B&B-in-the-woods (80 acres of woods, to be exact). Part of the contemporary home is an antique shop, and every room is furnished with antiques. One of the five guest-rooms is called the "Old-Fashioned Room," where guests can sleep on a 1790 four-poster, cannonball rope bed complete with feather tick mattress. The other furniture in the room is cherrywood, dating from the 1830s.

Other Silver Creek B&B recipes:
Pecan Pull-Apart Sticky Buns, page 86
Michigan Fruit Cup with Pecan Sauce, page 112
Pecan Waffles, page 145
Fantastic Brownies, page 200

Kolaches

Ingredients:

2-1/4 cups potato water
1/2 cup sugar
2 teaspoons salt
1 package dry yeast
2/3 cup butter or margarine, melted
2 eggs (or 4 yolks)
6-1/2 to 7 cups flour

Apricot Filling:
1 package dried apricots
Sugar

Poppy Seed Filling:
1 pound poppy seeds, ground
1 cup sugar
1/2 cup light corn syrup
Maple flavoring to taste
4-6 tablespoons cream

Prune Filling:
1 pound dried prunes
1/2 cup sugar
1/2 teaspoon cinnamon

> For the dough: Make potato water by boiling peeled potatoes in water. Remove potatoes. Dissolve yeast in a small amount of the lukewarm potato water.
> In a large bowl, mix well the melted butter, sugar, salt, cooled potato water and eggs.
> Add dissolved yeast mixture and flour. Beat until the dough shines.
> Place in a warm room and let rise until dough has doubled (1-1/2 to 2 hours).
> Form dough into balls and place on a greased cookie sheet. Let rise again about 20 minutes.
> Depress the center of each ball at least twice using the forefingers of both hands. Place filling in the depression. Then let dough rise again about 10 minutes.
> Brush dough carefully with a well-beaten egg. Sprinkle on a streusel topping, if desired (1/2 cup flour, 1/2 cup sugar and enough shortening to make a crumbly mixture).
> Bake in a 375 to 400 degree oven for 12 to 15 minutes or until golden brown. Brush lightly with butter. Cool on a rack.
> For Poppy Seed Filling: Grind a small amount of seeds at a time in the blender. Mix all ingredients in a saucepan. Bring to a boil, stirring constantly. Store in the refrigerator.
> For Prune Filling: Cook prunes in water until soft. Drain, remove pits (buy the prunes with pits because pits add flavor) and mash. Add sugar and cinnamon and mix well.
> For Apricot Filling: Soak apricots overnight in enough water to cover. Simmer until soft. Drain any remaining water. Mash apricots. Add sugar to taste. Cool before using.

from **The Old World Inn**
331 South Main Street
Spillville, Iowa 52168
319-562-3739

This inn and Czechoslovakian restaurant are in an 1871 former general store in this town of 450, home of Czech composer Antonin Dvorak and the setting of Patricia Hampl's book, "Spillville." Innkeeper Juanita Loven opened the from-scratch restaurant (kolaches are popular) in 1987 after renovation of the building, and she also opened three guest-rooms upstairs. Thousands visit the unusual Bily Brothers clocks and Dvorak collection here.

Lemon Yogurt Bread

Ingredients:

    3 cups flour
    1 teaspoon salt
    1 teaspoon baking soda
    1/2 teaspoon baking powder
    3 eggs
    1 cup vegetable oil
    1-3/4 cups sugar
    2 cups lemon yogurt
    1 tablespoon lemon extract

> Sift the dry ingredients. Set aside.
> Lightly beat the eggs in a large bowl.
> Add oil and sugar. Cream well.
> Mix in yogurt and extract.
> Spoon into two well-greased loaf pans.
> Bake at 325 degrees for one hour.

from **Walden Acres**
Rural Route 1, Box 30
Adel, Iowa 50003
515-987-1338

Yogurt keeps this bread moist and makes it "healthy." And the bread is as good with tea as it is with breakfast, says Innkeeper Phyllis Briley. As an added bonus, it freezes well.

Phyllis is taking advantage of that freezer to have something on hand to go along with the breakfast entrees served to more and more guests who are finding their way two miles off Interstate 80 to this 40-acre retreat.

Phyllis, an antique dealer, and Dale, a semi-retired veterinarian, opened their home as a B&B in 1984, sort of by accident. So many interstate travelers were finding out that the Brileys would board horses overnight that the Brileys decided they might as well board the owners, too, and save the owners the 20-mile trip to Des Moines. Guests who come horseless are welcome, too, and stay in one of three guest-rooms. They enjoy fishing in the private lake, hiking, sledding, skating or staying in by the fire.

Another Walden Acres recipe:
Pumpkin Puff Pancakes, page 139

Lighthouse Bread

Ingredients:

- 6 cups whole wheat flour
- 6 cups unbleached white flour
- 2 tablespoons dry yeast
- 1/2 cup powdered buttermilk
- 1/2 cup soy flour
- 1 cup wheat germ
- 3 teaspoons cinnamon
- 2 teaspoon salt
- 1/2 teaspoon baking soda
- 1/2 cup nuts
- 1 cup raisins and/or apple chunks
- 7 cups hot water

> Dissolve yeast in some of the water (read package directions about temperature of water).
> Mix six cups of flour and all other ingredients. Then add the remaining flour.
> Spoon the dough into four non-stick loaf pans which have been oiled slightly and sprinkled with corn meal. Cover dough with a towel and allow it to rise until doubled in size by setting the pans on top of the oven, set at 300 degrees.
> Increase oven temperature to 360 degrees and bake the bread for about 30 minutes.

from **Big Bay Point
Lighthouse B&B**
#3 Lighthouse Road
Big Bay, Michigan 49808
906-345-9957

Twenty-six miles northwest of Marquette and about three miles east of the little town of Big Bay is this lighthouse, perched 60 feet above Lake Superior and clearly at the end of the road. When the brick lighthouse went into operation in 1896, it housed three families. Today, the lighthouse has six guest-rooms, 7.5 bathrooms and is home to Buck Gotschall and his guests.

In 1961, the U.S. Coast Guard sold the lighthouse and other buildings and 4,500 feet of Superior frontage. Three owners and substantial renovation later, Buck bought it for a B&B with x-c ski and corporate fitness packages in mind. Buck opened the B&B in late 1986. His concern for health and fitness is reflected in this bread, which has no sugar, no fat and no refined flours. "This recipe is forgiving and encourages experimentation," he said.
Guests get a chance to talk wth him and each other in the kitchen over breakfast before going into the Huron Mountains for hiking and x-c skiing.

Pennsylvania Dutch Kuechels (Raised Donuts)

Ingredients:

    1 package dry yeast
    4 eggs, slightly beaten
    1-3/4 cups sugar
    1 cup butter, softened
    2 cups evaporated milk, warmed
    1/2 cup lukewarm water
    1 tablespoon salt
    10 cups flour

Also:

    Vegetable shortening for frying
    Powdered sugar

> Dissolve yeast in lukewarm water.
> Mix all ingredients except flour.
> Make a "well" in the flour and mix in the above mixture.
> Turn the dough out on a floured board and knead for five minutes.
> Place dough in a greased bowl, cover and set in a warm place until it has doubled in size.
> Break off pieces two inches in diameter. Let the pieces rise again, covered, until doubled.
> For each doughnut, pull the dough out from the center so that the center is thinner.
> Heat shortening in a deep skillet or deep-fat fryer to 365 degrees. Drop in doughnuts and fry until golden brown.
> Remove from fryer and drain on paper towels. Sprinkle with powdered sugar.

Makes 4 dozen

from **The Collier Mansion**
1072 West Third Street
Dubuque, Iowa 52001
319-588-2130

Innkeeper Mary Fitzgerald vividly remembers her mother's hot, homemade doughnuts as Mary grew up in Pennsylvania. She likes to make her guests' stay in this 1895 Queen Anne mansion equally unforgettable. This home was built by a Dubuque lumberman, Robert Collier, who chose oak, birch and African mahogany to feature in columns, stairway and floors. Located in Dubuque's historic district, the Fitzgeralds offer three guest-rooms furnished with antiques. Visitors are treated to breakfast in the dining room or on the veranda, cooked by Mary and served by Paul and some of their three children, before heading out for a day of greyhound racing, riverboat rides, antique hunting or museum-going.

Prune Bread

Ingredients:

1 cup vegetable oil
2 cups sugar
3 eggs, slightly beaten
1 junior 7-1/2 ounce jar prune (or plum or apricot) baby food with tapioca
2-1/2 cups plus 1 tablespoon flour
2 teaspoons baking soda
1 cup buttermilk
1 teaspoon salt
1/2 teaspoon cinnamon
1 teaspoon vanilla

> Dissolve soda in buttermilk.
> Add salt and cinnamon to flour.
> Mix ingredients in order given, adding dry ingredients alternately with the buttermilk and soda. Mix thoroughly. Add vanilla.
> Pour into two greased loaf pans or four small greased loaf pans.
> Bake for 30 minutes at 350 degrees, then reduce temperature to 325 and bake another 30 minutes. (If using small pans, reduce the time at each temperature to 20 minutes.)

from **The Jackson Street Inn**
210 South Jackson Street
Janesville, Wisconsin 53545
608-754-7250

Innkeeper Ilah Sessler finds this recipe goes well with fruit, and summer guests may find themselves treated to fresh raspberries from Sessler's raspberry patch. The garden is just one of the benefits of this huge home. While raising their four children here, they rented out rooms to workers hired for extra shifts at the local GM plant, so they've had their home open to the public in one form or another for more than 30 years.

Their B&B opened in 1983. The four large guest-rooms are done in antiques and guests have a central sitting room and refrigerator. Downstairs, guests can enjoy the TV and fireplace in the living room. A full breakfast is served family-style in the sunny dining room at a time arranged the night before.

Another Jackson Street Inn recipe:
Apple Butter, page 90

Grandmother's Poundcake

Ingredients:

1 cup butter
1-2/3 cups sugar
5 eggs
2 cups flour
1/4 teaspoon vanilla or almond extract

> Work the butter until it's creamy.
> Beat in sugar, vanilla and eggs, adding eggs one at a time.
> When the mixture is creamy, fold in the flour with a spoon.
> Spread the batter in a buttered and floured loaf pan.
> Bake for 90 minutes at 300 degrees.

from **FitzGerald's Inn**
160 North Third Street
Lansing, Iowa 52151
319-538-4872

"This is a recipe that has been in my family for years. I can remember being able to help with the mixing. Then we'd all fight over the bowl," said Innkeeper Marie FitzGerald. "It has a great aroma while baking - the smell is as delicious as the taste." Pound cake, simple to make, does not require any more work to serve. It's rich and dense and Marie serves it often with tea in the afternoon to arriving guests.

Summer guests find that the large front porch, complete with restored gingerbread trim, is a fine place on which to enjoy their tea. Guests often find themselves "out back" as well -- the home sits at the bottom of a hill, and the terraced backyard leads up to a grand view of the Mississippi and riverbluffs. Since FitzGerald's Inn opened in 1987, some guests have had family or friend reunions at the inn, since Marie and Jeff live next door and guests have the place to themselves.

Another FitzGerald's Inn recipes:
Banana Soup, page 105

Pumpkin Poundcake

Ingredients:

- 3 cups sugar
- 1 cup vegetable oil
- 4 eggs
- 1-1/2 teaspoon salt
- 1 teaspoon cinnamon
- 1 teaspoon nutmeg
- 2 cups cooked pumpkin
- 3 cups flour
- 2 teaspoons baking soda
- 1 cup favorite nuts and/or raisins, optional

> Combine ingredients in the order listed.
> Add 1 cup nuts and/or raisins, as you desire.
> Pour into a greased pan. "I use an angel-food pan to make a pretty ring."
> Bake at 350 degrees for one hour.

from **Driscoll's for Guests**
1103 South Third Street
Stillwater, Minnesota 55083
612-439-7486

"This is one of many sweets served with spiced cider, herbal tea and coffee," said Innkeeper Mina Driscoll. "It's available all afternoon to guests checking in." She sets it next to the parlor fireplace. "It lasts a long time - if you can keep people away!" This is a hearty, heavy cake, and she also claims that "the pounds go with the cake, not on you!"

Mina knows the hospitality of the B&B business, being a veteran B&B traveler herself. "I've been staying in them for 20-some years," mostly in England and Ireland. She is an avid bicyclist and met plenty of interesting folks staying in the B&Bs after her day's biking.

In 1985, she officially opened her Victorian Stillwater home as a B&B of her own. She'd tried it earlier, but was ahead of her time: "Nobody had heard of them." Guests have their choice of three guest-rooms and when and where to be served breakfast. Stillwater, the birthplace of Minnesota, is located about a half hour from the Twin Cities, on the St. Croix River.

Other Driscoll's for Guests recipes:
Cider to Sit Around With, page 20
Oo-Hoo's Strawberry-Rhubarb Jam, page 100

Fresh Rhubarb Bread

Ingredients:

2-1/2 cups flour
1/2 cup pecans or walnuts, chopped
1 teaspoon baking powder
1/2 teaspoon salt
1/4 teaspoon nutmeg
1 teaspoon baking soda
1-1/4 cups buttermilk
1/2 cup vegetable oil
1 large egg
1 cup brown sugar
2 teaspoons vanilla
1-1/2 cups rhubarb, coarsely chopped and ends trimmed

> Mix the flour, nuts, baking powder, salt and nutmeg in a large bowl.
> Dissolve the soda in the buttermilk. Beat together buttermilk, egg, oil, brown sugar and vanilla.
> Stir buttermilk mixture into dry ingredients just until moistened. Batter will be lumpy.
> Fold in rhubarb.
> Bake at 350 degrees in two greased loaf pans for 45-50 minutes or until the top is golden brown.

from **The Inn at Cedar Crossing**
336 Louisiana Street
Sturgeon Bay, Wisconsin 54235
414-743-4200

"In the springtime and early summer, fresh rhubarb is available at the Farmer's Market, a block away," said Terry Wulf, innkeeper. Everything in town is just a block away from this inn, which is in an 1884 downtown building in one of Sturgeon Bay's two historic districts. This building was built like a European market, with shops at street level and the merchant's quarters upstairs. In 1985, Terry bought it and turned it into an inn like those in Europe and Quebec's French Quarter. Now, nine guest-rooms upstairs have country decor, antiques, cozy comforters and down pillows.

Other Inn at Cedar Crossing recipes:
Apple Yogurt Coffeecake, page 30
Surpise Muffins, page 58
Zucchini Chocolate Nut Bread, page 88
Nectarines with Cream Anglaise, page 113
Hot Apple Crisp, page 192
Crispy Caramel Corn, page 202

BJ's Sticky Buns

Ingredients:

1 package refrigerator breadsticks
1/3 cup sugar
1 tablespoon cinnamon
1/4 cup plus 2 tablespoons butter, melted
1/4 cup light corn syrup
2 tablespoons brown sugar
1/3 cup raisins
1/3 cup light cream or milk
1/3 cup walnuts, chopped (optional)

> Mix 1/3 cup sugar and cinnamon. Set aside.
> Pour 2 tablespoons melted butter into a 9 x 1-1/2-inch round baking pan. Swirl butter to coat pan. Drizzle light corn syrup into pan. Sprinkle brown sugar, raisins and walnuts on top of syrup and butter mixture.
> Separate but do not uncoil breadsticks. Dip the coils into remaining butter, then roll in the sugar and cinnamon mixture. Place coils flat in the pan.
> Pour light cream/milk over the coils.
> Bake in a 350-degree oven for 25-30 minutes.
> Let the pan stand for three minutes. Loosen the sides and invert on a warm plate.

Makes 8 servings

from **The Red Gables Inn**
403 North High Street
Lake City, Minnesota 55041
612-345-2605

Innkeeper Bonnie Saunders devised these buns, rich and sweet, using the time-saving refrigerator dough. They are part of a large breakfast buffet she and Bill set out every morning between 8:30 and 9. Guests may eat beside the fire in the dining room or on the screened-in porch.

The Saunders opened their B&B in the fall of 1987 in Lake City, the Mississippi River town where waterskiing was invented. They moved from Thousand Oaks, Calif., specifically to convert this elaborate 1865 home into a four guest-room inn.

Other Red Gables Inn recipes:
Brown Cream and Fruit, page 107
River Run Sausage 'n Eggs on French Toast, page 157

Pecan Pull-Apart Sticky Buns

Ingredients:

1 package dry yeast
1/4 cup lukewarm water
1/4 cup vegetable oil
1 cup milk, scalded
1/3 to 1/2 cup sugar
1 teaspoon salt
1 egg
1 cup water
3 to 3-1/2 cups flour
3 cups pecans, chopped
2 cups brown sugar
1 cup butter or margarine, melted

Topping:
1 cup brown sugar
3 tablespoons water
3 tablespoons butter
3 tablespoons white corn syrup

> Dissolve yeast in 1/4 cup lukewarm water.
> In a separate large bowl, mix scalded milk, oil, sugar and salt. Cool to lukewarm.
> Add yeast, egg and 1 cup water to cooled milk mixture. Beat with a mixer.
> Blend in the rest of the flour to form a soft dough.
> Place in a greased bowl. Cover. Let rise in a warm place until double (about one hour).
> In a greased bundt pan, sprinkle 1 cup pecans on the bottom.
> Set out three bowls: #1 - 2 cups brown sugar; #2 - 2 cups pecans; #3 - melted butter.
> When dough has risen, pinch off a piece the size of a walnut. Dip into butter, sugar, back into butter, then into pecans. Place the ball of dough in the bottom of the bundt pan.
> Continue until the bundt pan is half full, leaving space between each ball of dough so it can double again when rising. Cover and let rise in a warm place.
> Bake at 325 degrees for 75 minutes. Let sit for 5 minutes, then invert rolls onto a plate.
> Cook the topping ingredients over medium heat, stirring until thick. Pour over rolls.

from **Silver Creek B&B**
4361 U.S. Highway 23 South
Black River, Michigan 48721
517-471-2198

"This is just a basic sweet dough I've been making for years," said Kim Moses, who got a brainstorm to add the brown sugar and pecans. Kim rises early in order to get this dough to rise twice before it becomes part of a huge breakfast, served from 9-11 each morning. (Cooks can substitute a frozen sweet dough if they aren't quite as energetic as Kim.)

Other Silver Creek B&B recipes:
English Muffin Loaf, page 76
Michigan Fruit Cup with Pecan Sauce, page 112
Pecan Waffles, page 145
Fantastic Brownies, page 200

Zucchini Chocolate Bread

Ingredients:

3 eggs
1 cup vegetable oil
2 teaspoons salt
2 cups sugar
3 cups zucchini, grated
1 teaspoon cinnamon
2 teaspoons baking soda
1/4 teaspoon baking powder
2 teaspoons vanilla
2-1/3 cups flour
1/2 cup unsweetened cocoa
1/2 cup nuts, optional

> Mix dry ingredients, including nuts.
> Mix eggs, oil and zucchini. Then add to dry ingredients.
> Pour into two mid-sized greased loaf pans.
> Bake at 350 degrees for 45 minutes.

from **Thorp House Inn**
4135 Bluff Road
Fish Creek, Wisconsin 54212
414-868-2444

It's hard to believe something with zucchini can taste so chocolatey, but guests at this inn never know there's squash in the bread unless they ask. Chocolate for breakfast? Why wait until the end of the day to enjoy this healthy bread? When Christine and Sverre Falck-Pedersen include it with muffins and fresh fruit for their guests, no one refuses!

The Falck-Pedersens are carrying on a long tradition of hospitality in this house. The original builder, Freeman Thorp, perished in 1903 when a steamer sank on Green Bay, and his widow, Jessie, opened the Victorian home to boarders in order to support herself. Eventually, cottages were added and other innkeepers owned it. Chris and Sverre bought it from owners of a local restaurant who housed their summer help there. After months of restoration and redecorating with antiques, lace curtains and embroidered linens, they opened four guest-rooms in August 1986.

Other Thorp House Inn recipes:
Fresh Cherry Muffins, page 51
Apricot Bread, page 69

Zucchini Chocolate Nut Bread

Ingredients:

3 eggs
2 cups sugar
1 cup vegetable oil
1 teaspoon vanilla
2 cups zucchini, grated
2 ounces unsweetened chocolate, melted
2 cups flour
1 teaspoon baking soda
1 teaspoon salt
1 teaspoon cinnamon
1 cup walnuts or pecans, chopped
1/2 cup chocolate chips

> In a large bowl, beat eggs until light.
> While beating, gradually add sugar, oil and vanilla.
> Stir in melted chocolate and zucchini.
> Mix dry ingredients. Add gradually to zucchini mixture, stirring after each addition.
> Stir in nuts and chocolate chips.
> Pour into two mid-sized greased loaf pans.
> Bake at 350 degrees for one hour or until a toothpick inserted in middle comes out clean.

from **The Inn at
Cedar Crossing**
336 Louisiana Street
Sturgeon Bay, Wisconsin 54235
414-743-4200

"Breakfast time is a great time for chocolate," says Innkeeper Terry Wulf.
"Despite its decadence, our guests can never resist it. This recipe is really
moist and oh-so chocolatey!" Besides that, it's a dandy way to make a dent in
the squashes with which Midwest gardeners are overwhelmed if they've
planted zucchini and can't pawn any more off on their neighbors.

Other Inn at Cedar Crossing recipes:
Apple Yogurt Coffeecake, page 30
Surprise Muffins, page 58
Fresh Rhubarb Bread, page 84
Nectarines with Cream Anglaise, page 113
Hot Apple Crisp, page 192
Crispy Caramel Corn, page 202

In the very appropriate words of Innkeeper Gloria Krys of the Urban Retreat, Ann Arbor, Michigan: "For André and me, nothing satisfies the way canning and preserving does. It's a link with the past, those mothers and grandmothers who spent time in the summer and fall putting up food for their families. Seeing rows of jars lining the pantry shelves gives us a sense of well-being and readiness for the cold winter months ahead. Sharing our bounty with our guests is just one more way of telling them, 'You are special -- we're glad you're here.' "

Preserves, Butters, Spreads & Sauces

Apple Butter

Ingredients:

3 quarts sweet apple cider
8 pounds well-flavored apples
2-1/2 cups brown sugar (firmly packed)
1-1/2 teaspoons ground cloves
2-1/4 teaspoons cinnamon
1-1/4 teaspoons allspice
1/2 teaspoon salt

> Reduce the cider by half (to 1-1/2 quarts) by cooking over moderate heat for about one hour.
> Quarter and core the apples.
> Add the apples to the cider. Cook until tender, stirring frequently.
> Work the apple mixture through a sieve to remove the peels.
> Return the puree to the kettle. Add sugar, spices and salt.
> Cook until very rich and thick, about three hours, stirring constantly. "This scorches easily!"
> Pour into hot, sterilized jars.

Makes 6-7 pints

from **The Jackson Street Inn**
210 South Jackson Street
Janesville, Wisconsin 53545
608-754-7250

"This takes a long time to make but it's worth the effort," said Innkeeper Ilah Sessler. Apples from the backyard at the Jackson Street Inn always go into Ilah's homemade, aromatic apple butter. Apples aren't the only thing worth crowing about in this backyard. First of all, there's a large garden and sometimes raspberries or other breakfast dishes will have come straight out of the garden. But most warm-season guests will remember this as the only Wisconsin (U.S.?) B&B where they can get in a few holes of golf before breakfast. Bob has put in a four-hole putting green out in back. Or guests can play a game of shuffleboard or horseshoes.

Bob and Ilah bought this huge 1899 home in 1956. Fortunately, the natural oak woodwork on the stairway, built-in cabinet and ceiling remains unpainted and gleaming. Sesslers have maintained the original leaded glass found in nearly every room. They have four large guest-rooms.

Another Jackson Street Inn recipe:
Prune Bread, page 81

Apple Cider Marmalade

Ingredients:

    5 cups firm apples, cored and slivered (unpeeled)
    1/4 cup apple cider
    7 cups sugar
    1 package powdered pectin
    1/2 cup orange rind, grated
    1/2 cup lemon rind, grated

> Prepare apples (food processor works well).
> Mix apples, cider, rinds and pectin in a saucepan. Bring the mixture to a rolling boil.
> Add sugar and stir until completely dissolved.
> Bring to a rolling boil again. Boil 65 seconds, stirring constantly.
> Remove the mixture from the heat. Cool for three minutes.
> Skim off any foam with a slotted spoon. Ladle into sterilized jars, cover and process in a hot water bath.

Makes about 10 cups

from **The Old Rittenhouse Inn**
Rittenhouse and Third
Bayfield, Wisconsin 54814
715-779-5111

Nothing could be more "Bayfield" than apples, says Innkeeper Mary Phillips, who, with husband Jerry, operates the Old Rittenhouse Inn and gourmet restaurant. Mary created this marmalade to take advantage of as much local produce as possible. Bayfield has such an abundance of apples, visitors to the annual Apple Festival each October crowd the streets of this lake-side town, eating caramel-covered apples, pies and other goodies.

The Rittenhouse staff serve this marmalade with homemade bread, as a topping on pancakes, and as a glaze for Rittenhouse Cheese Pie, Mary said. It and other preserves account for nearly 4,000 jars made in 1987 and purchased in Bayfield or through a growing mail-order business.

Mary and Jerry opened this 1890 mansion as a B&B in 1974, long before the concept reached the Midwest. Today, the inn has nine guest-rooms and has gained fame for dinners and Sunday brunch, open to the public.

Other Old Rittenhouse Inn recipes:
Maple-Poached Pears, page 114
Lake Superior Trout Meuniere, page 171

Apple Cider Sauce

Ingredients:

    2 cups apple cider
    1-1/2 cups light corn syrup
    1/2 cup sugar
    1/2 cup butter
    Juice and grated rind of two lemons
    1/2 teaspoon nutmeg
    1/4 teaspoon ginger
    2 tablespoons cornstarch

> Dissolve the cornstarch in a little of the cider.
> Mix all ingredients in a large saucepan. Cook over medium heat until thickened, stirring constantly.
> Serve warm over pancakes, waffles, ice cream, apple dumplings or apple, pumpkin or mince pie.

Makes about 3 cups

from **The Apple Orchard Inn**
Rural Route 3, Box 129
Missouri Valley, Iowa 51555
712-642-2418

It's not surprising to find apple pie with warm apple cider sauce on the menu at the Apple Orchard Inn, which sits on a hillside overlooking the Boyer Valley amid hundreds of apple trees. Innkeeper Electa Strub says she always has some of this sauce on hand and "I'm always finding new uses."

Electa and John Strub have "retired" to this three guest-room B&B in an historic farmhouse. They are veteran travelers themselves, taking to the road and air after careers in educational administration. They finally returned to Electa's hometown after living and working in Alaska and seeing the USA in their motorhome. They wanted to settle down again, but not to have time on their hands.

Opening the B&B in this valley, which reminds them of Ireland, seemed to be a perfect option. They enjoy meeting other travelers and swapping travel stories. Electa loves to cook and has opened a small restaurant in the inn serving "country-style gourmet" fare. John has taken to restoring the orchard on their 26 acres, planting 300 apple trees the first year.

Another Apple Orchard Inn recipe:
Gingerbread Waffles, page 143

Blueberry Jam

Ingredients:

        4-1/2 cups fresh Michigan blueberries
        4 teaspoons lime peel, grated
        1/4 cup lime juice
        6-1/2 cups sugar
        2 pouches (6 ounces) liquid pectin

> Place washed and drained blueberries in a large kettle. Add peel, juice and sugar.
> Stirring constantly, bring mixture to a full rolling boil.
> Remove from heat and stir in pectin.
> Pour hot mixture into hot, sterilized half-pint jars, leaving a quarter- inch "head space."
> Adjust caps and bands. Process 15 minutes in a boiling water-bath canner.
> Remove from the bath and let the jars cool in a draft-free area.
> When cooled, remove the bands, wash the jars, label and store.

Makes about 14 half-pint jars

from **The Urban Retreat**
2759 Canterbury Road
Ann Arbor, Michigan 48104
313-971-8110

"Try topping a toasted bagel with cream cheese and this jam - wonderful!"
said Innkeeper Gloria Krys. "Adding lime to blueberry jam seems to
intensify the blueberry flavor. Using pectin allows you to cook the fruit
less than in traditional jam recipes - you end up with a jam that has chunks
of whole fruit in it."

Guests at this B&B, which Gloria and her husband, André Rosalik opened in
1986, are often treated to Michigan produce. They also get to soak up
plenty of peace and quiet. Both Gloria and Andre work full-time in the
mental health field, and they rent out only one of their two guest-rooms at a
time. They have found their B&B sideline to be satisfying and enjoyable.

"Initially, we had considered opening a B&B as a retirement activity," Gloria
said. "Since that is a long way off, we decided not to postpone the fun." And
it has been fun, she said. "We have met some terrific people."

Other Urban Retreat recipes:
Dried Cherry Scones, page 61
Peach-Orange Marmalade, page 95

Mom's Chili Sauce

Ingredients:

6 pounds ripe tomatoes
1/2 pound (1 bunch) celery, chopped
1/2 quart onions, chopped
2 green peppers, chopped
1/3 tablespoon ground cloves
1/2 tablespoon dry mustard
1 stick cinnamon
1 pound brown sugar
1/8 cup salt
1/2 quart cider vinegar

> Scald and peel tomatoes. Then core, slice and cook them for 15 minutes.
> Drain off half the juice. Add the chopped vegetables and simmer for 90 minutes.
> Tie spices in a cloth bag. Add them with the remaining ingredients to the tomato mixture.
> Simmer, stirring regularly, until the sauce is reduced by one-half to a thick consistency.
> Remove spices. Ladle into hot sterilized jars and seal.

Makes 3 pints

from **The Wisconsin House**
Stagecoach Inn
2105 East Main Street
Hazel Green, Wisconsin 53811
608-854-2233

"We at the Inn use this as a condiment for scrambled eggs at breakfast," said Innkeeper Betha Mueller. "And at supper, Swedish meatballs are prebaked and simmered in the sauce with a touch of wine jelly for three to four hours." Betha and John also like it as a condiment with fresh pork roast.

These two childhood sweethearts first fell in love with innkeeping while running a B&B in Galena, Illinois, nine miles away. But they always wanted an original old inn, Betha said, so in 1985 they bought this 1846 stagecoach stop in Hazel Green, once a busy lead mining community. Today, the five guest-rooms and downstairs community rooms sport a picture-perfect country decor. John and Betha also enjoy serving family-style suppers on Fridays and Saturdays, and they provide entertainment, as well as good food.

Another Wisconsin House Stagecoach Inn recipe:
John's Deviled Eggs, page 162

Peach-Orange Marmalade

Ingredients:

    20 medium peaches ("Red Havens are best")
    10 cups sugar
    6 oranges

> Scald, peel and dice peaches.
> Squeeze juice from oranges.
> Remove membrane from inner peel of oranges. Process peels in a food processor or grinder until they're in small pieces, or chop finely with a knife.
> Combine ingredients in a large ceramic or stainless steel bowl. Cover and let stand overnight.
> Set over heat, stirring until sugar dissolves.
> Bring to a boil and cook over moderate heat for one hour (or until clear and thick), stirring frequently to prevent scorching.
> Pour into hot, sterilized pint jars, leaving a quarter-inch "head space."
> Adjust caps and bands. Process 15 minutes in a boiling water-bath canner.
> Remove from the bath and let the jars cool in a draft-free area.
> When cooled, remove the bands, wash the jars, label and store.

Makes about 7 pint jars

from **The Urban Retreat**
2759 Canterbury Road
Ann Arbor, Michigan 48104
313-971-8110

This may not be the quickest recipe Innkeeper Gloria Krys has in her collection, but it's worth the extra time and effort. "Even we when are busy, we make sure to put aside time each year to put up this marmalade. Opening a jar on a cold, snowy morning brings the color and flavor of August to the breakfast table."

No matter the season, guests receive a liberal dose of relaxation here, in a quiet neighborhood. Next door is the County Farm Park, with 127 acres of meadowland and walking and jogging trails. Gloria and husband André Rosalik typically rent only one of their two guest-rooms at a time, so guests are assured of a quiet visit and personal attention. Both rooms, named after favorite aunts, are done in antiques and old-fashioned wallpaper.

Other Urban Retreat recipes:
Dried Cherry Scones, page 61
Blueberry Jam, page 93

Orange Butter

Ingredients:

1/4 pound (1 stick) butter, softened
1 3-ounce package cream cheese, softened
1/3 cup powdered sugar
2 tablespoons orange rind, grated
1 tablespoon frozen orange juice concentrate

> When butter and cream cheese are at room temperature, mix all ingredients until smooth.
> Serve at room temperature topped with a sprinkle of extra orange rind.
> Store, covered, in the refrigerator. If this is crumbly after refrigeration, bring to room temperature and mix again.

from **The Griffin Inn**
11976 Mink River Road
Ellison Bay, Wisconsin 54210
414-854-4306

Bran muffins were invented to go with this butter, say guests staying at the Griffin Inn in the northern part of the Door Peninsula. It's also wonderful on other muffins and hot breads.

Laurie and Jim Roberts have added lots of special recipes to the Griffin Inn's menus since they bought this inn one day in 1986 and had 10 guests arriving the next day. "Trial by fire," Laurie calls it, and she laughs about it now. But they've made it through with flying colors and have been able to do much more for the inn and their guests than just get by. Upstairs in the 10 guest rooms, handmade quilts cover the old-fashioned brass, iron or antique wood beds. Downstairs, the living area around the fireplace or the redecorated dining room are popular gathering places for guests. Popcorn is served downstairs after guests return from dinner.

Located on a quiet road, the inn has a gazebo and five acres of grounds with a sports court for tennis or basketball, and lots of lawn for croquet. Boating and swimming in Green Bay waters at Ellison Bay are just a block or two away. Two miles away is Newport Beach State Park, which has hike-in camping and beautiful stretches of sandy Lake Michigan beaches.

Other Griffin Inn recipes:
Apple Squares, page 29
Old-Fashioned Oats Coffeecake, page 37
Sesame Whole Wheat Pancakes, page 140
Apple-Bacon-Cheddar Bake, page 146

Pesto

Ingredients:

A sinkful of washed and dried, fresh basil leaves
4 to 8 ounces good olive oil
1 garlic clove, crushed
1/4 cup Parmesan cheese
2 tablespoons olive oil
1 tablespoon butter
A few pine nuts or walnuts, optional

> Step One: After you have planted, tended and harvested the basil (or purchased fresh basil at the Farmer's Market), grind the basil with as little oil as possible to make a paste. Use the blender or, better yet, the food processor.
> Freeze it in ice cub trays. When frozen, transfer the cubes to a bag for frozen storage.
> Step Two: To use the concentrate, defrost a cube. For each cube, add the garlic clove, Parmesan, nuts, olive oil and butter.
> Add the completed pesto to hot pasta. Or layer it with butter and cream cheese to make a cheese log for tea time. Or mix it with more Parmesan cheese and use it in an omelette (you may want to omit garlic). Or add a thin layer when making lasagna. Or spread on a thin layer before the last rise and baking of homemade French bread loves. Or mix with Parmesan and cheddar cheeses, place 1 teaspoon in a pre-made crescent roll, roll up the dough and bake as directed, serving hot.

from **The Canterbury Inn**
723 Second Street SW
Rochester, Minnesota 55902
507-289-5553

Innkeepers Jeffrey Van Sant and Mary Martin have so many ideas to use this pesto that they can't name the best. A frequent guest, however, claims the hot pesto-filled crescent roll was a peak experience for him.

The afternoon tea here is a peak experience for everyone. The homemade treats -- down to the sourdough crackers on which the paté, pesto-cream cheese or baked brie are served -- are so tasty and plentiful that some guests skip dinner (but not breakfast, which continues the fantastic fare).

Other Canterbury Inn recipes:
Canterbury Eggs Benedict, page 119
Minnesota Wild Rice Waffles, page 144
Sourdough Crackers (Lavosch), page 212

Raspberry Sauce Au Chambord

Ingredients:

    1 pint raspberries, fresh or fresh-frozen (not in syrup)
    3/4 cup sugar
    1/4 cup white wine
    1/2 cup heavy cream
    2 tablespoons Chambord raspberry-flavored liqueur

> Combine raspberries, sugar and wine in a saucepan.
> Cook over medium heat until mixture boils, then let simmer for five minutes or until raspberries are soft.
> Remove from heat and puree in food processor or blender.
> Strain out the seeds and squeeze out all the juice.
> Return the juice to stove and simmer slowly until slightly thickened (15 minutes is not unusual).
> Add heavy cream and Chambord. Simmer five minutes more.
> Serve warm or at room temperature over pancakes, French toast, waffles or cheesecakes.

Makes about 1-1/2 cups

from **The Collins House**
704 East Gorham Street
Madison, Wisconsin 53703
608-255-4230

"Squeeze in a little lemon juice if you like, or orange juice - there are ways to play with it," said Innkeeper Barb Pratzel, who sometimes adds a little wine after cooking to add the wine flavor back in. Barb concocted this sauce as a present for her catering partner, who loves French toast.

Guests at the Collins House will find this sauce on the table Saturday mornings, when a pancake of some kind always is served. "We find guests don't touch the maple syrup anymore," Barb said. She makes five times the recipe in order to use it in Collins House Custom Catering, a business she began after she and Mike opened their B&B in 1985.

The Pratzels have renovated a 1911 historic home of Prairie School architecture. Perched above Lake Mendota, the building had been used as apartments and, since the '50s, as office space. Their four guest-room B&B features breakfast in the sunrooms overlooking the lake.

Other Collins House recipes:
Potato Pancakes, page 168
Pumpkin Pie, page 187

Aunt Clara's Strawberry Preserves

Ingredients:

    2 cups strawberries, crushed
    2 cups strawberries, whole
    4 cups sugar

> Boil the crushed berries with 2 cups sugar. After the mixture comes to a rolling boil, cook for 10 minutes, stirring occasionally.
> Add the whole berries and remaining sugar. Boil mixture for another 10 minutes, stirring occasionally.
> Pour into a large bowl to cool. Stir often (the faster the steam gets out, the thicker the jam will be).
> Let stand for 24 hours before putting jam in sterilized jars and sealing with wax (or processing in a hot water bath).

Makes five 8-ounce jars

from **Evergreen Knoll Acres
Country Bed & Breakfast**
**Rural Route 1, Box 145
Lake City, Minnesota 55041
612-345-2257**

Innkeeper Bev Meyer received this recipe from her Aunt Clara. Her aunt lived on a small farm near Red Wing, Minn., where she had her own strawberry patch. She also started weaving rugs there, weaving until she was more than 90 years old. Today, the chunky strawberry jam gets raves from guests who spread it on Bev's toasted, homemade bread.

Some guests have worked up quite an appetite by breakfast time, since they've been up and out in the barn watching the milking. "When we opened our B&B, we hoped to get city people who maybe hadn't been on a farm before, or maybe had a grandparent on a farm and remembered visiting them when younger," Bev said. "Some people are enthusiastic about the farm tour. We milk at 4:30 a.m. and 4:30 p.m., so if they get here too late for the evening milking, they probably won't get up that early to watch -- but they still can see how everything works."

Other Evergreen Knoll Acres recipes:
Streusel Coffeecake, page 42
Strawberry Cheddar Cheesecake, page 179
Fresh Fruit Pizza, page 205

Oo-Hoo's Strawberry-Rhubarb Jam

Ingredients:

  1 cup fresh rhubarb, cut in chunks
  1 cup fresh strawberries
  1 small package dry strawberry gelatin
  1 cup sugar

> Combine all ingredients.
> Slowly heat over low heat until sugar and gelatin are dissolved and the fruit is soft. Keep stirring.
> The fruit provides the liquid.
> Chill thoroughly before serving.

Makes about 2 cups

from **Driscoll's for Guests**
1103 South Third Street
Stillwater, Minnesota 55083
612-439-7486

This was a recipe handed down orally to Innkeeper Mina Driscoll by her great-grandmother. "Her name that is used by the family is 'Oo-Hoo,'" said Mina. "She was still rosemaling furniture at age 90." Oo-Hoo is also the person who collected all the family antiques now enjoyed by the guests.

Mina makes this jam from her garden-fresh produce. She often serves it with steaming-hot homemade popovers and rolls. Her guests may enjoy breakfast in bed, on the wicker-filled screened porch, by the parlor fireplace or in the dining room. Their decision often depends on the season and whether they want privacy or to chat with other guests.

Guests find plenty to talk about in this Victorian home. It was built just after the Civil War by a dentist who worked in downtown Stillwater. He insisted on using his new-fangled gravity furnace for three long winters, during which time most people used stoves. And for most of those three long winters, his wife and daughters moved into an inn in town.

Comfort is no longer a problem in this home. Guests are welcomed at check-in with tea and they may use the porch or the parlor, which has a working fireplace and piano.

Other Driscoll's for Guests recipes:
Cider to Sit Around With, page 20
Pumpkin Poundcake, page 83

Spicy Tomato Jam

Ingredients:

   5 pounds firm red tomatoes
   5 pounds sugar
   1 lemon
   1 tablespoon whole cloves
   1 stick cinnamon

> Skin and cut up the tomatoes. Slice the lemon very thinly, then cut slices in half.
> Combine all ingredients in a large pot. Simmer slowly until thick, about 45 minutes, stirring frequently, especially when it begins to thicken.
> Remove spices.
> Pour jam in sterilized jars and seal at once.

Makes about four 6-ounce jars

from **Greystone Farms B&B**
770 Adam's Church Road
East Troy, Wisconsin 53120
414-495-8485

"This jam will surprise you," said Innkeeper Ruth Leibner. "It has the flavor of strawberry jam with a hint of spiced apples." And it's a godsend for gardeners who find themselves with an abundance of ripe tomatoes.

"My children still remember the aroma that would fill the house from the simmering pot on the stove," Ruth said. Today, guests at Ruth and Fred's Greystone Farms are tantalized by the good smells coming from the kitchen. A huge country breakfast is one of the draws here. Others are the exceptionally good drinking water, the tree swing in the front yard and the peace-and-quiet along this country road.

And that's to say nothing of the farmhouse itself, which the whole family pitched in to help restore before opening their B&B in 1986. The Leibners built an addition for themselves, then wallpapered all the rooms. The four upstairs guest-rooms have antique ceilings and double beds (one is an 1860s Eastlake, which came with the house), and they're all done with country prints and antiques.

Other Greystone Farms recipes:
Danish Puff Cake, page 36
Overnight Pancake Batter, page 137
Fried Tomatoes, page 170

There's nothing fruitless about the Upper Midwest. The bounty here is tremendous: apples, pears, cherries, grapes, several kinds of berries and more. For many of us, many a memorable summer day has been spent out in the jackpines with only a pail, surrounded by chipmunks and millions of blueberries. Even if we can't pick our own, the sweetness of fruit as an appetizer, side dish, entree or dessert is a wonderful way to start the day. In cold weather, as these recipes show, we don't give up the fruit -- we just turn up the heat and bake, boil or broil it!

Fruits

Stuffed Baked Apples

Ingredients:

    4 medium, tart baking apples
    2 ounces ground almonds or filberts
    1 tablespoon orange or hazelnut-flavored liqueur (or wine)
    1/2 cup apricot jam
    1 tablespoon water
    4 English biscuits or macaroons, crushed

Also:

    Whipped cream
    Toasted, slivered almonds

> Scoop out the center of the apples.
> Make a paste with the ground nuts and liqueur. Stuff the center of the apples with the paste. Score at the top with a knife so as not to split the skin when baking. Place in a shallow, ungreased baking pan.
> Bake in a 350 degree oven for 25-30 minutes. (Do not overcook or they will fall apart).
> Remove from oven. Heat the apricot jam with water. Brush the tops with the heated jam.
> Sprinkle the crushed biscuits or macaroons over the top. Garnish with whipped cream and toasted, slivered almonds. Serve hot.

Makes 4 servings

from **Bluff Creek Inn**
1161 Bluff Creek Drive
Chaska, Minnesota 55318
612-445-2735

"Ordinary" baked apples become very appealing to the eye, nose and taste buds in this recipe, said Innkeeper Anne Karels. Breakfasts at the Bluff Creek Inn often include this fruit dish as one of several attractive courses, served on white flowered china in front of the pot-bellied stove.

Guests have their choice of five upstairs rooms in this brick farmhouse. It was built in 1860 on land granted by President Abraham Lincoln before Minnesota became a state. Over the years, some of the land has gone for highways or the railroad, and the house was foreclosed upon during the Depression. But today it still sits on a gravel road surrounded by farmland and flowers. Guests love to use the porch or tree swings.

Other Bluff Creek Inn recipes:
Candlelight Coffee for Two, page 22
Special Valentine Meringues, page 189

Hot Cooked Apples

Ingredients:

1 apple per person
1/2 cup apple cider or juice
Cinnamon, nutmeg or allspice
Cream cheese, softened
Pure maple syrup

> Peel and slice one apple per person. "Granny Smith or Ida Reds are my favorite as they stay firm and hold their shape."
> Pour juice or cider over the slices. Sprinkle with spice of choice.
> Cover and cook until "fork tender." Serve steaming hot or set aside and microwave when ready to serve.
> Combine cream cheese with a small amount of maple syrup.
> Place a tablespoon or so of sweetened cream cheese in the center of the hot apples just before serving.

from **A Country Place**
Route 5, Box 43
North Shore Drive
South Haven, Michigan 49090
616-637-5523

The maple syrup-sweetened cream cheese adds a wonderful, complementary flavor and really dresses up the fruit, and it will keep in the refrigerator for up to two weeks. Lee Niffenegger also said the cooked apples can be served inside crepes for an entree. Just remember to reserve the juice and add a little sugar and cornstarch and then a pat of butter.

A hot, spicy apple is just the thing for a brisk fall or cold winter morning at this B&B, located an easy walk from sandy Lake Michigan beaches. Lee, a native South Havenite, is happy to direct guests to winery tours, fishing, boating, golfing, antiquing, fruit picking or sightseeing.

Guests are always happy to come back to her B&B at the end of their day. In the summer, the deck is a favorite gathering place. In cooler months, guests will get to talking around the fireplace in the living room. They all are surprised by the table settings for breakfast, which Lee changes daily using a large collection of china and table linens.

Other A Country Place recipes:
Blueberry Streusel Coffeecake, page 33
Easy A.M. Cinnamon Rolls, page 72

Banana Soup

Ingredients:

  6 bananas
  Juice of 1 lemon
  1 teaspoon cinnamon
  1/2 teaspoon nutmeg
  1/2 teaspoon ground cloves
  1/2 cup milk
  1/2 cup raisins
  1/2 cup walnuts

Also:

  Heavy cream, whipped

> Combine everything except the raisins and walnuts in a blender. Blend on high speed for 3 minutes or until well blended.
> Chill for an hour (or it can be served as is). Pour into bowls or parfait glasses. Spoon raisins and nuts onto the soup in bowls or glasses.
> Top with a scoop of whipped cream.

from **FitzGerald's Inn**
160 North Third Street
Lansing, Iowa 52151
319-538-4872

This may be called a soup, but this thick breakfast concoction is almost a smoothie blender drink that's healthy as well as quick and tasty. "We made this up one weekend when friends were visiting and we couldn't get over how good it was," said Innkeeper Marie FitzGerald.

Marie serves this to guests in the dining room of this 1863 rivertown home. She and husband Jeff, an interior decorator, bought what was a neglected and ailing home after falling in love with the small riverbluff towns of McGregor and Lansing. Jeff's parents, Margaret and Chris FitzGerald, also live in Lansing and also run a B&B there. They were very helpful in restoration work, which included refinishing parquet floors and tin ceilings.

Five guest-rooms opened to visitors in 1987. Marie and Jeff live next door with their children, and Marie comes in every morning to serve a homemade breakfast from 8 to 10. Egg dishes feature herbs from the inn's garden.

Another FitzGerald's Inn recipe:
Grandmother's Pound Cake, page 82

Broiled Sunshine

Ingredients:

1 large grapefruit
1 tablespoon real maple syrup
Cinnamon

> Cut the grapefruit in half and remove seeds. Cut around each section for easy removal.
> Broil the halves five to 10 minutes until the top of the fruit or rim starts browning.
> Remove the fruit from the oven or toaster oven and put in small bowls.
> Drizzle the top of both halves with real maple syrup.
> Sprinkle with cinnamon. Serve warm.

Makes 2 servings

from **Victorian Treasure B&B**
115 Prairie Street
Lodi, Wisconsin 53555
608-592-5199

"This dish turns anti-grapefruit people into true believers and is sure to bring warm sunshine -- or at least the feel of it -- into everyone's winter breakfast." Innkeeper Linda Bishop discovered this after a family friend sent her and husband Joe Costanza a case of Florida grapefruit one Christmas. She saw a similar recipe using oranges and sugar, so she experimented until the modifications were right.

Linda and Joe settled in Wisconsin in 1984 and found this 1897 Queen Anne mansion after much searching for the perfect potential inn. Linda had been a substitute innkeeper in Massachusetts, and she and Joe had dreamed of running their own inn, so it was just a question of when and where.

The home, built by an entrepreneur and state senator, had been a single-family dwelling for 60 years and retains many original fixtures. Another owner did much of the restoration work in the 1970s, and Joe and Linda did some more before opening four guest-rooms in 1987. They are offering unusual biking, antiquing and picnicking packages and feature monthly speakers on local attractions and history.

Another Victorian Treasure B&B recipe:
Currant News Pie, page 203

Brown Cream and Fruit

Ingredients:

    1/2 teaspoon vanilla
    2 tablespoons light brown sugar
    3/4 cup sour cream
    1 tablespoon Grand Marnier liqueur, optional
    2 oranges
    2 firm, red apples
    2 bananas
    2 to 3 tablespoons berries (raspberries/blackberries are good) or nuts and raisins

> Combine vanilla, brown sugar, sour cream and liqueur in a small container. Mix thoroughly and set aside.

> Peel the oranges. Remove as much of the "white" as possible. Cut each orange section into three or four pieces.

> Wash and chop apples into bite-sized pieces.

> Peel bananas and cut in half lengthwise, then into pieces.

> Combine the cut fruit in a large bowl and toss gently so the juice from the oranges will stop the apples and bananas from discoloring.

> Add the brown cream mixture and toss gently again.

> Top with fresh berries and refrigerate until ready to serve.

Makes 8 servings

from **The Red Gables Inn**
403 North High Street
Lake City, Minnesota 55041
612-345-2605

Necessity was the mother of this recipe. Innkeeper Bill Saunders discovered that the winter fruit supply in a small Midwest town can't rival that of California, from whence he and Bonnie moved to open this B&B. A winter fruit dish, then, had to use the fruit available, be good for their guests, and be unusual and a bit rich.

The Saunders believe a stay in this restored 1865 mansion is good for their guests as well. The home was built by a wealthy wheat merchant who came to the shores of Lake Pepin on the Mississippi River to relax and enjoy the four seasons, as guests do today.

Other Red Gables Inn recipes:
BJ's Sticky Buns, page 85
River Run Sausage 'n Eggs on French Toast, page 157

Creamy Fruit Dressing

Ingredients:

    1 8-ounce package of cream cheese, softened
    1/4 cup fresh orange juice (increase slightly if Grand Marnier is omitted)
    2 tablespoons sugar
    1/2 teaspoon ginger
    Splash of Grand Marnier liqueur

> Combine all ingredients in the blender until completely smooth. ("I sometimes use frozen orange juice concentrate for a stronger orange flavor.")
> Placed chilled fresh, seasonal fruits (strawberries, raspberries, melon balls, kiwi fruit, blueberries and bananas are especially good) in frosted stemmed goblets or bowls. Pour the dressing over the fruit and garnish with fresh geranium leaves. Serve immediately.

from **The Inn at
Wildcat Mountain**
Highway 33
Ontario, Wisconsin 54651
608-337-4352

"This dressing I created for summertime out-of-doors breakfasts, and it's always a hit," said Patricia Barnes, innkeeper of the 1908 home of one of Wisconsin's earliest ginseng growers, Charlie Lord. His success at growing this root and shipping it to Far East markets enabled him to build what appears to be Tara (one of the guest rooms is named "Scarlett's") or another plantation estate on the Kickapoo River. Lord had heard the railroad was going to go through Ontario, so he took a chance on constructing a hotel, complete with horsehair-filled pillars from Tennessee.

The railroad never did run through town, but guests at the Inn at Wildcat Mountain now get the benefit of Lord's efforts. The inn still has the long front lawn, the river still runs through the back of the property, and the horsehair is still in the pillars. Guests have the use of the grounds (perfect for a croquet match or just a stroll), two porches and a reading room downstairs. Upstairs, they can choose from three guest-rooms.

The Inn shares a name with Wildcat Mountain State Park, only two-and-a-half miles away from the peak and a half-mile from the park. The park offers hiking, camping and x-c skiing among some of the prettiest limestone bluffs in this scenic "Hidden Valleys" region of Wisconsin.

Other Inn at Wildcat Mountain recipes:
Mother's Fresh Rhubarb Cake, page 39
Light Chocolate Ambrosia Roll, page 195

Frozen Fruit Frappé

Ingredients:

  2 small cans frozen orange juice concentrate
  Juice from 2 lemons
  1 16 or 17-ounce can crushed pineapple
  2 to 3 bananas
  1 cup ginger ale or 7-Up
  1 cup sugar

> In a blender, blend all ingredients until smooth.
> Pour into stemmed glasses or dessert bowls and freeze.
> Remove from freezer about 30 minutes before serving.

Makes about 8 servings

from **Victorian Bed &
Breakfast Inn**
425 Walnut Street
Avoca, Iowa 51521
712-343-6336

This thick, refreshing fruit dish is often served at this B&B along with an entree and breakfast meat. Innkeeper Jan Kuehn serves breakfast in the dining room of this 1904 Queen Anne Victorian home, where guests get a chance to talk. Built by a successful contractor, the home is predictably one of the finest in the community. The pine woodwork is impressive, and guests marvel over the detailed columns, large windows and craftsmanship.

Jan and Gene bought this operating inn in September 1987 and their feet haven't touched the ground since. In addition to the B&B, lunches and dinners are available to guests and the public by reservation. The Kuehns find their guests are often local residents or their families and friends or travelers between Omaha (45 miles away) and Des Moines (90 miles). The four guest-rooms are done in antiques, and Jan says antique buffs will love the 14 antique shops in Walnut, Iowa, just five miles away.

Another Victorian B&B Inn recipe:
French Toast Puff, page 128

Golden Fruit Cup

Ingredients:

- 1/4 to 1/2 cup sugar
- 1 tablespoon lemon juice
- 2 tablespoons cornstarch
- 1 20-ounce can pineapple chunks, drained (reserve juice)
- Juice and grated rind of one orange
- 1 11-ounce can mandarin oranges, drained
- 2 apples, peeled and cut into bite-sized pieces
- 1 to 3 bananas, optional

> Stir sugar and cornstarch together in a saucepan. Blend in 3/4 cup pineapple juice, lemon juice, orange rind and orange juice (hint: grate the orange rind, then peel off all membranes and remove the seeds, then put the whole orange in the blender and use it all).
> Cook over medium heat, stirring constantly, until the mixture thickens and boils.
> Boil and stir constantly for one minute.
> While the sauce is hot, pour it over the pineapple chunks, apples and mandarin oranges. Then refrigerate it all, uncovered, for several hours or overnight.
> Serve in crystal dishes. Add some banana slices, if desired, and garnish with parsley, a maraschino cherry or, in the summer, a marigold blossom.

Makes 12-16 servings

from **Cedar Knoll Farm**
Route 2, Box 147
Good Thunder, Minnesota 56037
507-524-3813

Innkeeper Mavis Christensen often serves this appealing fruit dish when summer fruits are not available. She notes that, without the bananas, it keeps well in the refrigerator for several days.

At Cedar Knoll Farm, a 138-acre working farm in the Minnesota River valley, guests are treated to a family-style, full country breakfast. Depending on the season, the day ahead and the guests, Mavis may serve ham, eggs, homefries, hotcakes, apple pie and homemade jam, or "a lighter menu" of muffins, pastries, fruit and omelettes. No one goes hungry here with an afternoon tea snack and even cookies or crackers before bedtime.

Another Cedar Knoll Farm recipe:
Frau Paquin's Egg Roll-Ups, page 163

Hot Fruit Compote

Ingredients:

Ingredients:
- 1 pound dried prunes, pitted
- 1 pound dried apricots
- 1 32-ounce can pineapple chunks
- 3/4 cup water (or partly drained pineapple juice)
- 1 large can cherry pie filling
- 1/4 cup sherry
- 1/2 cup sugar

> Place dried fruit in the bottom of a baking dish. Layer the pineapple on top.
> Mix the water, sherry and sugar. Pour it over the fruit.
> Spread the cherry pie filling on top.
> Bake uncovered at 350 degrees for 30 minutes.
> Serve warm. For extra richness, pour over some heavy cream or add a generous dollop of whipped cream.

Makes 12-15 servings

from **The Inn on the Square**
3 Montgomery Street
Oakland, Illinois 61943
217-346-2289

This warm, rich fruit compote is flavorful anytime of the year, but it seems especially appropriate in the winter as it's served in front of a huge fireplace. Guests here have a full breakfast in the Windowpanes Tea Room, patterned after Colonial Williamsburg. It also is open for lunches.

Caroline and Max Coon, who have lived in the area for 30 years, thought it was a shame that the old house was sitting empty. The original house had been expanded since it was built in the mid-1800s, and Caroline put her mind to finding some use for it. In 1986, she and Max bought the place to open a tea room and a small business.

Today, the house has four shops selling gifts, flowers, local crafts, antiques and women's dresses, plus the tea room and B&B. B&B guests have three antique-filled guest-rooms upstairs, plus their own library for reading, TV or working puzzles. In the evening, they are welcomed with a glass of wine at fireside for a get-acquainted chat.

Michigan Fruit Cup with Pecan Sauce

Ingredients:

1 favorite Michigan melon, scooped into balls
2 cups strawberries, washed and halved
2 cups blueberries, washed
Other fruit of choice to equal 6 cups total

Pecan Sauce:
1/2 cup sour cream
1/4 cup powdered sugar
1/4 cup orange juice
1/3 cup pecans, chopped

> Combine the fruits.
> Mix the ingredients for the sauce. Pour it over the fruit.
> Refrigerate for at least one hour before serving in fruit bowls or parfait glasses.

Makes up to 12 servings

from **Silver Creek B&B**
4361 U.S. Highway 23 South
Black River, Michigan 48721
517-471-2198

At her B&B, Kim Moses has nearly every edible, wild berry Michigan can produce -- raspberries, blackberries, thimbleberries, blueberries and strawberries. Kim's home is located on 80 acres of forest that adjoins 5,200 acres of federal land, located between Harrisville and Alpena.

Year 'round, the land is attractive to her guests. A number of hiking and cross-country ski trails begin at her door and cut through the woods. This part of the state is loaded with clear springs bubbling up and starting brooks and streams. Hikers often see deer and wild turkey. There's plenty of old-fashioned outdoor fun, too. Guests are welcome to enjoy a campfire on the property. In fall and winter, a hayride or sleighride can be arranged.

No matter what the season, guests should climb the hill nearby (before breakfast) for a view of Lake Huron. The hill is the highest elevation in the county and climbing it is no easy task for those who've just feasted on this fruit cup, a banana drink, French toast, ham, egg casserole and sticky buns.

Other Silver Creek B&B recipes:
English Muffin Loaf, page 76
Pecan Pull-Apart Sticky Buns, page 86
Pecan Waffles, page 145
Fantastic Brownies, page 200

Nectarines with Cream Anglaise

Ingredients:

2-1/2 cups milk
1/2 cup sugar
Zest of 1 orange (grated peel)
3 tablespoons cornstarch
2 eggs
1 tablespoon orange-flavored liqueur
12 nectarines, sliced

> Combine milk and zest of orange and scald. Set aside.
> Mix sugar and cornstarch and beat in eggs.
> Slowly whisk hot milk into egg mixture. Return mixture to heat.
> Stir while cooking until thickened.
> Remove from heat and add liqueur. Chill.
> To serve, spoon the chilled sauce on a dessert plate. Top with sliced nectarines, fanning them around the plate.

Makes 12 servings

from **The Inn at
Cedar Crossing**
336 Louisiana Street
Sturgeon Bay, Wisconsin 54235
414-743-4200

Fruit is always included in the breakfast offered at The Inn at Cedar Crossing, and this fruit plate is as pretty as it is refreshing. Eye-appeal is important throughout the inn. In the lobby area downstairs, guests can see the original tin ceiling from the 1880s.

Upstairs, Innkeeper Terry Wulf has spent a lot of time with renovation and decorating. Apartments were converted to put in nine guest-rooms, and each has its own "country" personality. Hand-woven rugs, stenciled walls and antique furnishings are used extensively.

Other Inn at Cedar Crossing recipes:
Apple Yogurt Coffeecake, page 30
Surpise Muffins, page 58
Fresh Rhubarb Bread, page 84
Zucchini Chocolate Nut Bread, page 88
Hot Apple Crisp, page 192
Crispy Caramel Corn, page 202

Maple-Poached Pears

Ingredients:

6 to 8 pears, peeled, cored and cut into quarters
1 cup maple syrup
1/2 cup orange juice
Juice from half of a small lemon
Rind from half of an orange, cut into julienne strips (all white removed)

Also:

Fresh mint, chopped

> Combine all ingredients, except the mint, in a saucepan.
> Bring the mixture to a boil, then reduce heat and simmer for 10 minutes.
> Cool slightly. Pour into a glass serving bowl or individual dishes. Garnish with mint.

Makes 4-6 servings

from **The Old Rittenhouse Inn**
Rittenhouse and Third
Bayfield, Wisconsin 54814
715-779-5111

"I wait all year to serve this recipe," said Innkeeper Jerry Phillips. About the end of August, Bayfield's pears turn golden yellow and are ripe. The combination with maple syrup is distinctive. "And don't even *think* of using anything but pure maple syrup in this one," he said.

Jerry and Mary Phillips opened this 26-room mansion in downtown Bayfield in 1974. They were both teaching music in Madison at the time they saw the house, and "our friends thought we were nuts." They bought it strictly because they fell in love with it, but the operation has since become one of Bayfield's largest and best-known businesses.

In addition to the nine guest-rooms at the Old Rittenhouse, two other B&Bs in town are operated through the Old Rittenhouse. Guests all meet at the main inn for a continental breakfast. Breakfast is open to houseguests only, and features homemade breads, preserves and fresh fruit such as this.

Other Old Rittenhouse Inn recipes:
Apple Cider Marmalade, page 91
Lake Superior Trout Meuniere, page 171

Poached Pears in Cranapple Juice

Ingredients:
    6 ripe pears
    2 cups cranberry-apple juice
    1/2 cup water
    1 large cinnamon stick

Also:
    Mint sprigs
    Lemon wedges

> Wash and peel the pears, leaving stems on.
> In a heavy saucepan, combine all ingredients. Bring to a boil uncovered.
> Reduce the heat and simmer until pears are tender, 20 to 30 minutes.
> Carefully lift the pears into a serving bowl. Discard the cinnamon stick.
> Bring the juice to a boil, reduce the heat, and simmer uncovered for 20 minutes. Juice should have boiled down to 1-1/2 cups.
> Pour juice over the pears. Refrigerate until well-chilled, turning occasionally. Serve garnished with mint sprigs and lemon wedges.

Makes 6-12 servings

from **The Old Holland Inn**
133 West 11th Street
Holland, Michigan 49423
616-396-6601

A well-tended pear hedge with plenty of fruit left Innkeeper Dave Plaggemars experimenting with recipes. He suggests serving this as part of a light breakfast or as a mid-afternoon treat with chilled wine or iced tea.

Breakfast guests here savor the pears along with French-roast coffee, served on china and table linens under 10-foot ceilings and original light fixtures. Fran, an art student, and Dave, a social worker and one-time sheriff's deputy, restored this 1895 home in one of Holland's historic districts. They opened the B&B in March 1986, and have four antique-filled guest-rooms upstairs. Downstairs, if you can pry the two cats away, you can sit in front of the original fireplace with an ornate heat-reflecting insert. In the summer, a deck invites leisurely breakfasts.

Other Old Holland Inn recipes:
Whole Wheat Apple Nut Oatmeal Muffins, page 45
Poppy Seed Orange Date-Nut Bread, page 75
Chilled Pineapple Peach Soup, page 210

Scandinavian Fruit Soup

<u>Ingredients:</u>

> 4 cups water
> 1 lemon, sliced very thinly
> 1 6-ounce package of dried apricots
> 1 8-ounce package (1 cup) light or dark raisins
> 1 teaspoon cinnamon
> 2 16-ounce cans sliced pears, with juice
> 2 16-ounce cans sliced peaches, with juice
> 1 16-ounce can red tart Door County cherries, drained

<u>Also:</u>

> Yogurt

> In a large kettle, place the first five ingredients. Cover and simmer for 30 minutes or until the lemon rinds are soft.
> Add canned fruit.
> Serve warm or chilled with a dollop of yogurt on top.

from **The White Lace Inn**
16 North Fifth Avenue
Sturgeon Bay, Wisconsin 54235
414-743-1105

Innkeeper Bonnie Statz came up with this recipe by starting with traditional recipes and experimenting. "We sometimes add an apple, making sure not to overcook it," she said. This recipe makes a lot of soup, but it can be kept in the refrigerator for four or five days. To reduce the recipe, Bonnie said to use 3 cups water, 1 lemon and half of everything else. Another change: "The apricots can be omitted for a less-sweet fruit soup."

No matter what version guests here are served, no one's complaining. In the winter, the soup is served warm, and in the summer, it's served chilled, along with warm, fresh-baked muffins and breads. There are other seasonal pleasures at this inn, as well. The gardens in the summer and fireplace in the main house in the winter are favorite wedding spots. Bicycles built for two are waiting out in front for spring, summer and fall guests. Guest-rooms have fireplaces or whirlpools, four-poster or walnut Victorian beds, and plenty of lacy linens and pillows.

Other White Lace Inn recipes:
Cherie's Spicy Pumpkin Muffins, page 55
Zingy Cheese and Egg Casserole, page 127

Eggs have long been standard breakfast fare. As might be expected at these B&B inns, amazing things are done with the ordinary, inexpensive, always-on-hand egg. From cheddar to chili peppers, the combinations are marvelous. Likewise, innkeepers have a way of making elegant creations out of what used to be rather mundane French toast, pancakes or waffles. Then there are some entrees that defy categorizing -- a German farmer's breakfast, fresh trout dishes, a spinach casserole, even elderberry blossom fritters. The secrets of those super-special B&B brunches are secrets no more!

Entrees

Baked Eggs

Ingredients:

10 eggs, beaten
1/4 pound fresh mushrooms, sliced
1/2 cup onion, chopped
4 slices uncooked bacon, diced
1/4 pound cheese - colby, farmers or cheddar, grated

Also:

Nutmeg
Tomato slices
Green pepper slices
Salsa, optional

> Combine all ingredients.
> Pour into a large, greased casserole dish.
> Sprinkle top with nutmeg.
> Bake at 325 degrees for 30 minutes or until the mixture bubbles and rises.
> Remove from oven and slice into four servings.
> Garnish each slice with tomato and green pepper. Salsa can be used on top, as well.

Makes 4 servings

from **Young's Island B&B**
Gunflint Trail 67-1
Grand Marais, Minnesota 55604
1-800-322-8327

This hearty egg dish, along with hot cranberry muffins and a fruit plate, is a perfect beginning for guests at this log cabin. No matter the season, they most likely are going to need energy for the day's x-c skiing, canoeing or hiking in this wild country that borders the Boundary Waters Canoe Area.

Ted, Barbara and son Joey join guests for breakfast at 9 a.m. The cabin looks out over Poplar Lake and its rocky shoreline and thick woods. Inside, guests are treated to breakfast on pink-flowered Haviland china and cranberry glasses. The Youngs have one guest-room available in their log cabin, which is heated with wood, adding to the northwoods feeling here. Young's Island B&B is located on an island in the middle of the 60-mile-long Gunflint Trail, a haven for canoeists, hikers, fishermen, cross-country skiers and dog sled mushers.

Another Young's Island recipe:
Cranberry Muffins, page 53

Canterbury Eggs Benedict

Ingredients:

6 English Muffins
1 dozen eggs
12 very thin slices of applewood smoked ham AND/OR
12 green tomato slices, 1/2-inch thick
Cornmeal
Bacon drippings

Blender Hollandaise:
3 eggs yolks
2+ tablespoons lemon juice
1/2 teaspoon salt
Dash hot pepper sauce
1/2 cup butter, melted

> For the Hollandaise sauce: put the first four ingredients in a blender and blend briefly.
> Add the melted butter to the blender contents while the butter is still bubbling and the blender is running.
> For Eggs Benedict: toast and butter the English muffins.
> Place a thin slice of warmed ham on each muffin. If using tomatoes, dredge the green tomato slices in cornmeal and salt and pepper and fry them slowly (for at least 10 minutes) in bacon drippings. Place the tomato slices on the English muffins.
> Top with a poached egg and about one tablespoon of the Blender Hollandaise sauce.

Makes 6 servings

from **The Canterbury Inn**
723 Second Street SW
Rochester, Minnesota 55902
507-289-5553

Innkeeper Jeffrey Van Sant's maternal grandmother, whose maiden name was Jeffrey and after whom the innkeeper is named, taught her the fried green tomato recipe. Jeffrey and co-innkeeper Mary Martin have added this interesting twist to classic Eggs Benedict. The Blender Hollandaise, they report, can be made ahead and refrigerated or frozen "and it never fails." To reheat it, heat only until it's lukewarm or it will bake and stiffen.

These two women looked long and hard before settling on Rochester for their B&B. After looking as far away as the Caribbean, they decided this town, with the Mayo Clinic and a large IBM office, would mean year 'round business. And busy they are. Special touches, like breakfast about anytime a guest wishes, and a reputation for great breakfasts have led to success.

Other Canterbury Inn recipes:
Pesto, page 97
Minnesota Wild Rice Waffles, page 144
Sourdough Crackers (Lavosch), page 212

Eggs Linné

Ingredients:

    3 tablespoons Creme Fraiche

    4 eggs

    Pinch of cream of tartar

    1-1/2 to 2 ounces Cantal cheese (or Havarti), sliced

Creme Fraiche:
    3 parts heavy cream
    1 part sour cream

> One day ahead, make Creme Fraiche: Combine creams by shaking in a jar. Leave at room temperature for about 24 hours, then refrigerate. (Cartons of Fleur du Lait brand Creme Fraiche are available in some grocery stores.)

> Carefully separate the eggs.

> Whip the egg whites with the cream of tartar until they are stiff.

> Spread the whipped whites in a flat, six-cup baking dish (10 x 6 x 2-inch oval or two-quart souffle dish).

> With a large spoon, make four "nests" evenly spaced in the egg whites.

> Carefully slide an egg yolk into each nest.

> Cover the entire dish with the thinly-sliced cheese. Then spread Creme Fraiche over all.

> Bake at 350 degrees for exactly 12 minutes (until eggs are set and cheese is melted).

> Serve onto plates, with one egg yolk in each serving.

Makes 4 servings

from **Linné Bed & Breakfast**
2645 Fremont Avenue South
Minneapolis, Minnesota 55408
612-377-4418

"Eggs Linné came about as a result of our attempt to serve ordinary eggs in an elegant manner," said Innkeeper Robert Torsten Eriksson. "The result is pleasing to both the eye and tastebuds -- puffy and golden brown. It looks grand on blue and white calico Staffordshire china."

These eggs are often a treat for weekend guests at this urban B&B, which Robert and his wife, Casey Higgins, opened in 1987. Whether weekend or weekday, seasonal fruits, fresh-squeezed juice, homebaked goods and fresh-ground coffee always are included. Breakfast may be served by the fireplace in the dining room, by the front window in the living room, or to the three guest-rooms upstairs.

Other Linné recipes:
Casey's Cream Scones, page 62
Plättar (Swedish Pancakes), page 138

Eggs Mornay

Ingredients:

1/4 cup butter, melted, plus 3 tablespoons
1/4 cup green peppers, chopped
1/3 cup onions, chopped
2 cups cooked, cubed ham, seafood or sausage
12 large eggs, beaten
4-1/2-ounce jar mushrooms, drained
2 cups soft bread crumbs
1/4 cup Parmesan cheese, grated
2 tablespoons fresh parsley, chopped

Mornay Sauce:
2 tablespoons butter
2 tablespoons flour
1 teaspoon chicken bouillon
1-1/2 cups milk
1/2 cup Swiss cheese, grated
1/4 cup Parmesan, grated

> Saute onion and green pepper in the 3 tablespoons butter until onion is crisp-tender.
> Add meat and eggs. Stir occasionally over medium heat until the eggs are firm but moist.
> Fold in mushrooms and remove from heat.
> For Mornay Sauce: in a saucepan, melt butter. Blend in flour and bouillon and cook until smooth and bubbly. Gradually add milk. Cook until mixture boils and thickens, stirring constantly. Add cheeses and stir until smooth.
> Fold scrambled eggs into sauce. Pour into a greased 12 x 8-inch baking dish.
> Mix bread crumbs, Parmesan cheese, 1/4 cup melted butter and chopped parsley. Sprinkle over eggs.
> Bake at 350 degrees for 30-35 minutes or until the topping is light golden brown and a knife inserted in the center comes out clean.

Makes 8-10 servings

from **The Rivertown Inn**
306 West Olive Street
Stillwater, Minnesota 55082
612-430-2955

"This is a great make-ahead dish," said Innkeeper Chuck Dougherty. "We serve it in individual souffle cups." Eggs Mornay is on the weekday menu here, when fewer guests allow Chuck and Judy the time to serve main entrees as well as a selection of home-baked pastries. The Doughertys took over this hilltop Stillwater home in May 1987. They plunged right into adding five bathrooms and four double whirlpools. The inn caters to honeymooners, anniversary couples, and business and pleasure travelers.

Other Rivertown Inn recipes:
Danish Kringle, page 35
Blueberry Buttermilk Oatmeal Pancakes, page 131
Pumpkin Custard Flan, page 198

Grandma's Iron Skillet Scrambled Eggs

Ingredients:

1 dozen eggs
1/2 pound bacon

> Cut the bacon into small pieces.
> Fry the bacon in an iron skillet. ("I can make these eggs in another skillet and they never taste as good as in the iron skillet -- even the kids say so.") The bacon should be almost, but not quite, crisp.
> Pour off the grease, saving 1 full tablespoon.
> While the bacon is frying, break eggs into a large mixing bowl. Beat them with a wire whisk until they're almost frothy.
> Pour the eggs into the warm iron skillet with the bacon "schnipples" and the tablespoon of bacon grease.
> Fry until almost set. Don't let the eggs get too dry.

Makes 6 servings

from **The Farm Homestead**
W1982 Kiel Road, Route 2
New Holstein, Wisconsin 53061
414-782-5421

"My mother always made these eggs for all the grandchildren on Sunday morning visits," said Marion Marsh, who runs this B&B with two sisters and three brothers on the family farm where they grew up. "Now, when we get together at the farm, the children still ask for those eggs."   Though Marion, a nurse, is concerned about the cholesterol content for her guests, guests request the eggs, anyway, and often say, "One time won't hurt."

Sections of this farm date back to 1858, about the time Marion's great-grandparents emigrated from Germany and settled here. Her father was one of 12 kids raised in this house. For his six offspring, the farmhouse was always a retreat from the city. Now it's a retreat others may share. In 1987, the siblings opened their family's farm home as a B&B. One brother lives nearby, and one of the family members is on hand when guests are present. Guests choose from five guest-rooms, though only four are rented at once, and each has some family heirlooms or antiques.

Another Farm Homestead recipe:
Elderberry Blossom Fritters, page 151

Basic Quiche Lorraine

Ingredients:

1-1/2 cups (6 ounces) Swiss cheese, grated
8 slices of crisp bacon, crumbled
9-inch unbaked pie shell
3 eggs
1 cup heavy cream
1/2 cup milk
1/2 teaspoon salt
1/4 teaspoon pepper
1/2 teaspoon dry mustard

> Brown the pie shell.
> Sprinkle cheese and bacon on the bottom.
> Beat the remaining ingredients together and pour into the pie shell.
> Bake at 375 degrees for 45 minutes or until firm and brown.

Makes 4-6 servings

from **The Quill and Quilt**
615 West Hoffman Street
Cannon Falls, Minnesota 55009
507-263-5507

To make this "basic" recipe not so basic, Innkeeper Denise Anderson advises substituting mushrooms and onions, or crab meat and fresh asparagus, for the bacon. Quiche is relatively simple to make, yet many guests are impressed by its puffed display and creamy flavors.

Guests at the four guest-rooms here also enjoy the evening social hour, when they have a chance to sample hors d'oeuvres and talk with each other. They also have an opportunity to talk with Denise and David Karpinski about innkeeping and historic renovation. A common area also is open to guests, as is the front porch and swing, the parlor with a fireplace, and the well-stocked library.

Other Quill and Quilt recipes:
Frozen Blueberry Muffins, page 49
Banana Bread, page 70
Raspberry Champagne Punch, page 188

Crustless Potato Quiche

Ingredients:

5 eggs, beaten
1 12-ounce package frozen hash brown potatoes, unthawed
1 cup cheddar cheese, shredded
1 large green onion, chopped
1/2 cup cottage cheese
1/4 teaspoon salt
1/8 teaspoon seasoned pepper
Dash of hot pepper sauce
Paprika
6 slices bacon, cooked and crumbled

> Combine everything except paprika and bacon and mix well.
> Pour the mixture into a greased 9-inch pie plate. Sprinkle with paprika.
> Bake in a 350-degree oven for 25 minutes or until the quiche is set.
> Remove from oven and sprinkle with bacon. Bake another five minutes.
> Remove from oven and let stand five minutes before serving.

Makes 6 servings

from **The Arman House**
2581 Grove Street
Boyne Falls, Michigan 49713
616-549-2764

Innkeeper Jackie Arman cooks this main dish up in her large country kitchen in the 120-year-old house. Year 'round guests need the energy its eggs, potatoes and cheese provide in order to ski, hike, swim or sail in this four-season recreational area of Michigan's northern Lower Peninsula.

Jackie and Norm restored the home after they retired from careers at Michigan State University. Norm was a groundskeeper, and their yard shows he hasn't retired completely. Jackie was a secretary in public relations, and she put those skills to good use once they opened the B&B in 1986. The second floor of the home has three guest-rooms, including a Spartan Room in MSU's green-and-white colors. Guests are invited to share the living room, which has a large fieldstone fireplace, and a bowl of popcorn and a mug of hot cider.

Another Arman House recipe:
Nine Bean Soup, page 211

Shirred Eggs

Ingredients:

2 tablespoons heavy cream per serving
1 egg per serving
Salt and pepper
Bacon bits, bread crumbs or grated cheese, optional

> For each serving, put 1 tablespoon cream in the bottom of a shirred egg dish or ramekin.
> Crack an egg on top of the cream.
> Top with another tablespoon of cream and salt and pepper. Sprinkle on a topping (bacon bits, bread crumbs, grated cheese, etc.), if desired.
> Bake at 400 degrees for four to five minutes. The egg white should be done and the yolk should be soft. (Use hot pads as the dishes get very hot.)

from **The Parsonage 1908**
6 East 24th Street
Holland, Michigan 49423
616-396-1316

Bonnie Verwys serves these Shirred Eggs with hot muffins or croissants, fresh seasonal fruit and a special blend coffee. When guests arrive, they're offered lemonade, tea, coffee or a wine cooler. After cross country skiing, they could warm up with a cup of hot mulled cider. There's never a food or beverage shortage around this B&B.

Bonnie opened the B&B with her daughter Wendy Westrate. Its name came about because the two-story home was built that year as a parsonage for the Prospect Park Christian Reformed Church.

Located in a residential neighborhood but close to restaurants, shops and Lake Michigan and Lake Macatawa, Bonnie thought it would be perfect for weekend getaways. Business travelers and visitors to Hope College also have found their way to the doorstep. Inside, much of the original oak woodwork and leaded glass remains in fine shape. Guests have their choice of four rooms upstairs, decorated in antiques. Downstairs, they are welcome to use the living room, glassed-in front porch or the garden patio.

Ham and Cheese Strata

Ingredients:

    12 slices white bread
    3/4 pound sharp cheddar cheese, shredded
    2 10-ounce packages frozen broccoli, cooked and drained
    1 pound baked ham, finely shaved
    6 large eggs, slightly beaten
    3 cups whole milk
    1 tablespoon minced onion
    1/4 teaspoon dry mustard

Also:

    Parmesan cheese, grated

> Cut 12 "doughnuts and holes" from the bread, using a doughnut cutter.
> Fit the rest of the bread, excluding crusts, in the bottom of a 15 x 9-inch greased baking dish.
> Layer the cheese over the bread, then the broccoli, then the ham.
> Place the bread doughnuts and holes on top.
> Combine the remaining ingredients and pour over the bread and layers.
> Cover and refrigerate at least six hours, or overnight.
> Sprinkle Parmesan cheese on top and bake uncovered at 350 degrees for one hour.
> Remove from oven and let the dish stand for 10 minutes before cutting into squares.

Makes 12 servings

from **The Gray Goose B&B**
4258 Bay Shore Drive
Sturgeon Bay, Wisconsin 54235
414-743-9100

This tasty breakfast casserole is part of what Jack Burkhardt calls "skip-lunch breakfasts," made by spouse and co-innkeeper Jessie. In addition to tasting great and looking attractive, the do-ahead portion allows Jessie to make it the night before.

Jack and Jessie opened this four guest-room B&B in 1987 after operating a Door County antique shop seasonally for 17 years. The home, just across the road from Green Bay, was built in the early 1860s to house the families of two men off to the Civil War. It took over a year for the Burkhardts to find the home, and they spent three months remodeling to accomodate guests. Opening a B&B was "a natural move" for them, says Jack, since Jessie loves to cook and they both enjoy meeting people and interior decorating.

Zingy Cheese and Egg Casserole

Ingredients:

    1 16-ounce loaf of French bread
    1-1/2 cups Monterey Jack cheese, grated
    1-1/2 cups cheddar cheese, grated
    1 8-ounce package cream cheese
    1 4-ounce can green chili peppers
    8 strips bacon, fried crisp and crumbled
    (Optional: 1 cup steamed, chopped broccoli, drained)
    10 eggs, beaten
    2 cups milk
    1/2 teaspoon dry mustard
    Dash of ground red pepper

> Cut the crusts off the French bread. Tear the bread into small pieces and place the pieces in the bottom of a greased 9 x 13-inch pan.
> Sprinkle the bread with the Monteray Jack, cheddar and small pieces of the cream cheese.
> Top with bacon, drained chilis and (optional) broccoli.
> In a separate bowl, beat eggs and stir in the milk, mustard and red pepper.
> Pour egg mixture over all. Cover and chill several hours or overnight.
> Bake uncovered in a 350-degree oven 55 to 60 minutes or until a knife in the center comes out clean or nearly clean.
> Let casserole stand 10 minutes before serving.

from **The White Lace Inn**
16 North Fifth Avenue
Sturgeon Bay, Wisconsin 54235
414-743-1105

"There are many 'egg bakes' around, but this one is really special. We use it for special occasions -- Easter or Thanksgiving breakfast, for instance," said Innkeeper Bonnie Statz. It's the White Lace Inn's use of chilis and red pepper that really give this dish its "zing."

Holidays in Door County have been popular since early steamers brought travelers up for summer stays. But it's not just for summer anymore, as visitors now come during four seasons. That's no surprise to Bonnie and Dennis, two Wisconsin natives. They considered New England and Michigan before renovating this former Knights of Columbus hall in 1982.

Other White Lace Inn recipes:
Cherie's Spicy Pumpkin Muffins, page 55
Scandianvian Fruit Soup, page 116

French Toast Puff

Ingredients:

1 cup flour
1 heaping teaspoon sugar
1 heaping teaspoon baking powder
Dash of salt
1 egg, beaten
About 3/4 cup milk
1 teaspoon vanilla

Also:

French bread
Vegetable oil for frying
Maple or other syrup, warm
Powdered sugar

> In a large bowl, mix flour, sugar, baking powder and salt. Stir with a spoon.
> Add milk and vanilla to the beaten egg. Then add the egg mixture to the flour mixture.
> Stir until the batter is well-mixed and rather thick (but if it's too thick, add more milk).
> Heat at least a half-inch deep of vegetable oil in a pan or fryer to 375 degrees (to test, dip a small piece of bread in the fat and if it browns too quickly, turn down the temperature and cool it down a bit).
> Cut the French bread diagonally in half-inch slices. Coat both sides with the batter.
> Drop the coated bread into the hot fat. In just a few seconds, turn and brown the second side. Bread should be medium brown.
> Drain on paper towels and serve with butter, warm syrup and a dusting of powdered sugar.

Makes 4 servings

from **Victorian Bed &
Breakfast Inn**
**425 Walnut Street
Avoca, Iowa 51521
712-343-6336**

In the early 1950s, Innkeeper Gene Kuehn had a delicious and different French toast aboard a train to the East Coast. For the next 30 years, he never found that special version. Then, in 1981, he came up with a recipe in the military files, 25 times bigger than the recipe above. It turned out just as he remembered, and guests at this five guest-room inn are just as enthusiastic about it when he and Jan serve it as he was 30-some years ago.

Another Victorian B&B Inn recipe:
Frozen Fruit Frappé, page 109

Pecan Stuffed French Toast

Ingredients:

4 ounces cream cheese
1 teaspoon vanilla
2 tablespoons sugar
3 tablespoons pecans, coarsely chopped
1 loaf day-old French bread, unsliced
3 eggs
1/4 cup water or milk
Butter-flavored shortening
Cinnamon and/or nutmeg

> Blend the cream cheese, vanilla, nuts and 1 tablespoon of sugar.
> Slice bread in about 1-1/2 inch slices. Then slice a pocket in the center of each.
> Spread about a tablespoon of cheese mixture in each pocket.
> Mix eggs, water and the other tablespoon of sugar.
> Dip the bread and let it soak in the mixture for a few minutes.
> Fry on a griddle or in frying pan in a little butter-flavored shortening until both sides are golden brown. Sprinkle with cinnamon or nutmeg. Serve with maple syrup or fruit sauces.

Makes 4 servings

from **The Victorian Swan
on Water**
1716 Water Street
Stevens Point, Wisconsin 54481
715-345-0595

The amounts in this variation on a classic breakfast entree can be changed to accommodate preferences (more cream cheese or nuts, for instance), said Innkeeper Joan Ouellette, who received a version of the recipe from one of her first guests.

Joan's been serving this rich dish since opening in 1986. She and her brother spent months restoring this 1889 home, uncovering black walnut parquet floors in the process. The house was originally built in another part of town and moved in 1938, when the owners took off a third story and cut the house in half to move it. Today, Joan has restored and opened four guest-rooms, plus large parlors and a TV room for guests' use.

Another Victorian Swan recipe:
Christmas Cranberry Wine, page 182

Austrian Apple Pancake

Ingredients:

    1/2 cup sugar
    1 teaspoon cinnamon
    2 tablespoons butter
    3 Granny Smith apples, peeled, cored and sliced 1/4-inch thick
    3 tablespoons flour
    3 eggs, separated
    3 tablespoons milk

Also:

    Sour cream, ice cream or maple syrup

> In a 10-inch skillet with a metal handle (if wooden or plastic, cover it with aluminum foil), melt the butter and swirl it over the entire bottom of the skillet.
> Combine cinnamon and sugar. Sprinkle over the melted butter.
> Add apple slices to sugar and cinnamon mixture and cook over low heat two to three minutes, until slices are well-coated.
> Beat flour, egg yolks and milk with a hand mixer or whisk.
> In a separate bowl, beat egg whites until stiff. Then gently fold egg yolk mixture in.
> Pour the batter over the apple slices, spreading it with a rubber spatula.
> Bake for 20 minutes at 400 degrees, until the pancake is brown and puffy.
> Remove from the oven. Loosen sides. Place a round plate over the skillet and turn the plate and skillet over, then lift off the skillet. Cut the pancake in wedges and serve with sour cream, ice cream or maple syrup.

Makes 6 servings

from **Die Blaue Gans**
(The Blue Goose)
9 S 265 Route 59
Naperville, Illinois 60565
312-355-0835

"When all the children (seven) were at home, this was a big treat on Sunday morning," said Innkeeper Molly Konrad, whose mother gave her the recipe. Now Molly serves it to guests during a candlelight breakfast. Many of the Konrads make up the Konrad Family Singers. Guests at this modern country home may hear them practice in the gazebo on a summer night. Molly has three guest-rooms, and the home is full of art and European decor.

Blueberry Buttermilk Oatmeal Pancakes

Ingredients:

1-1/4 cups old-fashioned oatmeal (not instant)
2 cups buttermilk
2 eggs, well beaten
1 cup flour
1 tablespoon sugar
1 teaspoon baking soda
1 teaspoon salt
1/4 cup butter, melted
1-1/2 to 2 cups blueberries, fresh or frozen

> Mix oatmeal and buttermilk. Add eggs.
> Combine the dry ingredients and mix them into the oatmeal mixture.
> Stir in the butter. Then gently stir in the blueberries (or add 8-12 blueberries to each pancake after pouring the batter on the griddle).
> Cook on a hot, greased griddle until bubbles show through. Flip and cook on other side until golden brown.

Makes 12 pancakes

from **The Rivertown Inn**
306 West Olive Street
Stillwater, Minnesota 55082
612-430-2955

Judy and Chuck Dougherty find an old breakfast standard, blueberry pancakes, can be significantly enhanced. "The use of oatmeal gives these pancakes a unique texture," Chuck said, as well as making them "heart-healthy." Judy and Chuck often experiment with recipes. She worked as a baker before getting a teaching degree and he has two years of cooking and baking courses, plus experience in food service jobs.

Since opening in May 1987, they renovated and redecorated the former home of John O'Brien, a prominent lumberman. (Stillwater, the birthplace of Minnesota, is a half-hour from the Twin Cities on the St. Croix River, once a major lumbering river.) Guests can choose from nine rooms and suites on three floors. Wine and cheese is served during a social hour that starts about 5:30, and may be held on the giant screened porch in the summer.

Other Rivertown Inn recipes:
Danish Kringle, page 35
Eggs Mornay, page 121
Pumpkin Custard Flan, page 198

Bran Pancakes

<u>**Ingredients:**</u>

    1 cup raw bran
    1 cup whole wheat or unbleached white flour
    1/2 teaspoon salt
    2 teaspoons baking powder
    1 tablespoon vegetable oil
    2 eggs
    1-1/2 cups milk
    Berries or chopped apples, optional

> Mix the first four dry ingredients.
> Add the rest of the ingredients and stir until well mixed.
> Pour onto a hot, greased griddle and cook until bubbles show through. Then flip and cook until the other side is golden brown.

Makes 9-10 pancakes

from **Chippewa Lodge B&B**
3525 Chippewa Lodge Trail
Lac du Flambeau, Wisconsin 54538
715-588-3297

These hot pancakes, perhaps containing fresh berries, are served to Chippewa Lodge guests in the large pine dining room. "We add lots of raspberries or blackberries from the woods -- it's a good complex-carbohydrate breakfast and guests love it," said Ann Rayson.

Breakfast is an informal affair here, as is the rest of the day. Rayson, Ben Bess and their three children spend 10 weeks here every summer. Guests can join them in fishing, boating, riding bikes, berry picking, swimming or just lounging. This former fishing lodge, which they bought complete with the old cola machine that stored bait, now hosts families instead of exclusively fishermen.

Guests pick from the four guest-rooms upstairs by the firmness of the mattress or proximity to the lake. The ping pong and pool tables downstairs get plenty of use on rainy days. Only the loons and bullfrogs make a racket at night. Chippewa Lodge B&B is open early June-late August. At other times, write 2555 Makaulii Place, Honolulu, HI 96816.

Another Chippewa Lodge recipe:
Berry Cake, page 32

Buckwheat Pecan Pancakes

Ingredients:

1/4 cup flour
3/4 cup buckwheat flour
1 teaspoon sugar
1/2 teaspoon baking soda
1/4 teaspoon baking powder
1/4 teaspoon salt
1/2 cup pecans, chopped
1-1/2 cups buttermilk
1 tablespoon vegetable (preferably safflower) oil

> Sift together flours, sugar, baking soda, baking powder and salt. Add pecans.
> In a separate bowl, mix buttermilk and oil.
> Add the dry ingredients to the liquid. Stir only until blended.
> Pour batter on a hot, lightly-greased griddle. Flip when bubbles show through.

Makes 4 generous servings

from **Hutchinson's Garden**
215 North High Street
Northport, Michigan 49670
616-386-5534

Innkeeper Kay Charter serves these light pancakes with butter and lots of homemade jam during a candlelight breakfast in the dining room of this Victorian inn. She and Jim have turned the former home of Northport's first doctor and a Civil War surgeon, Stephen Hutchinson, into a three guest-room inn. They opened their B&B in 1986.

The home, built in 1867, is surrounded by tall beeches and oaks and a native stone wall. All three guest rooms are on the second floor and overlook the gardens, from which flowers are placed in the rooms every day (the B&B is open May through October, so that's entirely possible). Guests are welcome to use the living room and enjoy afternoon chocolate coffee by the fireplace.

Bicycles are available for guests to use to explore Northport's mill pond, shops, marina and Lake Michigan beaches. Located on the Leelanau Peninsula, this B&B is close to Leelanau State Park, an historic Indian village, a fishing town and the Sleeping Bear Dunes National Lakeshore.

Corn Pancakes

Ingredients:

    3 eggs
    1/2 cup milk
    1 teaspoon baking soda
    2-1/2 cup flour
    2 teaspoons sugar
    1 tablespoon baking powder
    1/2 teaspoon salt, optional
    1 16 or 17-ounce can whole kernel corn (reserve and measure liquid)
    Enough water when, with liquid from canned corn, makes 2 cups
    4 tablespoons shortening, melted

> Beat eggs and stir in milk, corn and water.
> Mix dry ingredients. Add liquids and stir gently. Add shortening.
> Pour batter onto a hot griddle. When bubbles show through, flip and brown the other side.

Makes 20 six-inch pancakes

from **Chase's B&B**
508 North Huron Avenue
Spring Valley, Minnesota 55975
507-346-2850

Innkeeper Jeannine Chase recommends serving these pancakes with jams or jellies. Guests at her B&B receive wild plum jam for a topping.

Jeannine and Bob opened their B&B in 1986 in this brick French second empire-style home, listed on the National Register of Historic Places. The home was built in 1879 at a cost of $8,000 by William H. Strong, a local banker. Considered one of the most handsome buildings in the area, it stayed in the Strong family for more than 60 years. Since then, it has served as a doctor's office, motel, rest home and antique shop.

Jeannine and Bob bought it in 1969 to raise their family in Southeastern Minnesota's bluff country. Five guest-rooms are available, all decorated in antiques that are for sale. In Grandma's Room, for instance, the furniture is Scandinavian style and the large bed is made out of a loom. Michele's Room has a hooded walnut bed, Scott's Room has a six-foot high oak bed and Shannon's Room has a four-poster canopy bed.

Cottage Cheese Blender Pancakes

Ingredients:

    1 cup cottage cheese
    6 eggs
    1/2 cup flour
    1/4 teaspoon salt
    1/4 cup vegetable oil
    1/4 cup milk
    1/2 teaspoon vanilla

Also:

    Powdered sugar
    Raspberry syrup

> Put all ingredients in a blender and blend thoroughly.
> Refrigerate for at least 12 hours.
> After removing from the refrigerator, stir batter only once.
> Pour pancakes onto a hot griddle. When bubbles show through, flip and fry the other side.
> Remove the hot, cooked pancakes. Roll them up on a wooden clothes pin or using your finger as a "mold."
> Dust with powdered sugar and serve with raspberry syrup.

Makes 6 servings

from **The Inn**
Wisconsin Avenue
Montreal, Wisconsin 54550
715-561-5180

Innkeeper Doree Schumacher makes this batter the night before serving a hearty breakfast to skiers who come to the Hurley-Ironwood area to take advantage of the western Upper Peninsula's generous snowfall. The snow and slopes are what originally drew Doree and Dick to Montreal, a small "company town" built by Oglebay-Norton iron mining company and now on the National Register of Historic Places.

The Schumachers and their sons had been skiing in the area for years. They eventually purchased this building, the former mine headquarters office where miners or their wives would line up to collect a weekly paycheck. Since the Schumachers opened a three-suite B&B in 1982, skiers have been lining up, instead. The area is also popular in the other three seasons.

Another Inn recipe:
Finnish Cakes, page 204

Kathy Cakes

Ingredients:

1 tablespoon wheat germ
1 tablespoon oat bran
1/3 cup cornmeal
2/3 cup flour
1/2 teaspoon salt
2 tablespoons sugar
2 teaspoons baking powder
1/4 teaspoon baking soda
1-1/4 cups buttermilk
3 tablespoons vegetable oil
1 egg

> Mix all the dry ingredients together in a large mixing bowl.
> Mix the egg, oil and buttermilk in a separate bowl or large measuring cup.
> Add the liquid ingredients to the dry, but do not mix. "Fold" the batter together -- never stir or beat -- until it's just blended with no dry areas in the mixture.
> On a pre-heated griddle (325 degrees), spoon out individual pancakes, spreading the batter to a uniform thickness.
> When small bubbles form on the uncooked surface, flip them and cook the other side.

Makes about 12 six-inch pancakes

from **The Stout Trout B&B**
Route 1, Box 1630
Springbrook, Wisconsin 54875
715-466-2790

"This is my breakfast staple," says Innkeeper Kathleen Fredricks. "If these pancakes are not known throughout the world, they certainly are found throughout Gull Lake Township!" She and Myke Carver serve these (sometimes with wild blueberries cooked right in) with Wisconsin butter, their homemade maple syrup and home-smoked bacon from a local grocer.

Guests need a good breakfast for a day in the open air here on Gull Lake, out in the country a few miles from Hayward. Guests can use the boats out in front, swim, fish, hike or x-c ski right out the door. The four remodeled guest-rooms upstairs have country furnishings.

Another Stout Trout recipe:
Peach Meringues, page 167

Overnight Pancake Batter

Also suitable for waffles!

Ingredients:

5 cups unbleached flour
1/3 cup sugar
1-1/2 teaspoons salt
1 package dry yeast
4 cups milk
1/2 cup butter or margarine
6 eggs

> Heat the milk and margarine until very warm (120-125 degrees).
> Combine flour, sugar, salt and yeast in large bowl. "I use a large covered kettle in case the yeast is spunky and rises up in the refrigerator."
> Add the warm liquid and eggs to the dry ingredients. Beat until smooth.
> Cover and refrigerate. This will keep up to four days. Stir in 2 tablespoons sugar after the second day to keep the yeast fed.
> Pour about 1/4 cup batter per pancake onto a hot griddle. Turn when edges look cooked and bubbles begin to break on the surface.
> For waffles: bake in a hot waffle iron until steaming stops.

from **Greystone Farms B&B**
770 Adam's Church Road
East Troy, Wisconsin 53120
414-495-8485

"These are wonderful with syrup and butter or a mixture of sliced strawberries -- sweetened, if you like -- and vanilla yogurt," said Ruth Leibner. "They are also very easy to work with and are very special when filled with fresh fruit and rolled."

Ruth and Fred Leibner moved to their 27-acre farm in 1962 in order to have some space to raise their six children. The farm has been traced back to 1839, when it was purchased from Wisconsin Territory. Today, with the kids grown and neighbors taking the hay off, the B&B and an antique and gift shop which Ruth runs are the major enterprises.

Other Greystone Farms recipes:
Danish Puff Cake, page 36
Spicy Tomato Jam, page 101
Fried Tomatoes, page 170

Plättar (Swedish Pancakes)

Ingredients:

    3 eggs
    1 cup heavy cream
    1 cup flour
    2 cups milk
    1/4 cup butter, melted
    1/4 teaspoon salt
    1 tablespoon sugar, optional

Also:

    Sugar-stirred lingonberries, or lingonberry or other preserves
    Shortening or vegetable oil

> In a mixing bowl, beat the eggs and cream.
> Sift in the flour. Beat the batter until smooth.
> Add the milk gradually. Stir in the melted butter, sugar and salt.
> Brush a frying pan, griddle or Swedish *plättpanna* with melted shortening or vegetable oil.
> Heat the pan -- don't start frying until it is well heated.
> Stir the batter just before using (the thinner, the better).
> On a frying pan or griddle, pour the batter in little rounds, turning the pan gently to spread the batter. On a *plättpanna*, place 2 tablespoons batter in each section.
> When the surface of the cakes starts to bubble and gets dry, turn quickly and cook the other side until golden brown.
> Transfer the little pancakes to a warm serving platter. Keep them uncovered in a warm oven until all the batter is used.
> Serve topped with preserves.

Makes 4 servings ("If you divide the recipe in half, use 2 eggs.")

from **Linné Bed & Breakfast**
2645 Fremont Avenue South
Minneapolis, Minnesota 55408
612-377-4418

Innkeepers Robert Torsten Eriksson and Casey Higgins make these thin pancakes in a cast-iron *plättpanna* brought to the U.S. by Robert's maternal grandmother when she immigrated. Sweden has special meaning for these two. They lived there for a time, and named their B&B for the pink-and-white flower called "twinflower" here. Their 1896 home was built by Swedish immigrants, skilled carpenters who carved and inlaid the wood.

Other Linné recipes:
Casey's Cream Scones, page 62
Eggs Linné, page 120

Pumpkin Puff Pancakes

Ingredients:

　2 eggs
　1 cup milk
　1/3 cup cooked or canned pumpkin
　2-1/3 cups buttermilk biscuit mix
　2 tablespoons sugar
　1/4 teaspoon each: cinnamon, nutmeg and ginger
　1/4 cup vegetable oil

Also:

　Maple syrup, warmed
　Pecans, optional

> Beat eggs about five minutes or until soft peaks form.
> In a separate bowl, blend milk and pumpkin.
> Add the remaining ingredients. Beat with a mixer until blended (it will be stiff).
> Thoroughly fold in beaten eggs.
> Drop stiff batter by tablespoons onto a hot, greased griddle. When puffed and browned, turn and cook on the other side.
> Serve with warm syrup and sprinkle with pecans (optional).

Makes about 15 three-inch pancakes

from **Walden Acres**
Rural Route 1, Box 30
Adel, Iowa 50003
515-987-1338

"I would describe this recipe as being a favorite from October through the chilly months," says Innkeeper Phyllis Briley. She knows of what she speaks. Served on heated plates with warm maple nut syrup and accompanied by sausages, the flavor and aroma embodies all that's wonderful about a Midwest autumn (except burning leaves).

Phyllis and Dale Briley have set up their own embodiment of the Midwest on these 40 acres near Des Moines. The two-story, Old English brick home was built in 1940 by Cleveland Indians pitcher Bob Feller for his parents. Feller made sure there was fine walnut woodwork, arched doorways and other marks of good craftsmanship. The barn, built by Feller's grandfather, was where Feller practiced pitching with his father. Today, Dale Briley, a semi-retired veterinarian, boards horses there, some of which come with their owners as B&B guests en route to horse shows.

Another Walden Acres recipe:
Lemon Yogurt Bread, page 78

Sesame Whole Wheat Pancakes

Ingredients:

1 egg
1/2 cup all-purpose flour
1/2 cup whole wheat flour
3/4 cup milk
2 tablespoons melted butter or vegetable oil
1 tablespoon brown sugar
3 teaspoons baking powder
1/2 teaspoon salt
Sesame seeds

> Whisk together all ingredients, except for the seeds.
> Pour batter in a lightly-oiled skillet. Sprinkle sesame seeds generously over pancakes before turning them to the second side.
> Stack pancakes on a hot plate and cover with foil. You may keep them warm in a slow oven until enough are done for serving.
> Serve with syrup and fruit.

Makes about 9 four-inch pancakes

from **The Griffin Inn**
11976 Mink River Road
Ellison Bay, Wisconsin 54210
414-854-4306

This recipe is a favorite to start out cross-country skiers who take advantage of the Griffin Inn's special x-c ski weekend packages, in which five meals are included. Innkeeper Laurie Roberts describes the pancakes as "hearty, rich and delicious," just the type of entree to start out skiers. And Door County has plenty of trails to get them warmed up.

The Griffin Inn was named in memory of The Griffin, said to be the first and largest wooden ship sailing the Great Lakes. It was built in the 1670s near Niagara Falls by French explorer Robert de LaSalle to ship furs. On September 18, 1679, the ship went down off Washington Island, located at the tip of Door Peninsula. No clues about the sinking were ever found.

Other Griffin Inn recipes:
Apple Squares, page 29
Old-Fashioned Oats Coffeecake, page 37
Orange Butter, page 96
Apple-Bacon-Cheddar Bake, page 146

Sourdough Pancakes

Ingredients:

1 cup flour, sifted
2 tablespoons sugar
1-1/2 teaspoons baking powder
1/2 teaspoon salt
1/2 teaspoon baking soda
1 egg, beaten
1 cup sourdough starter (see recipe with Sourdough Coffeecake, page 41)
1/2 cup milk
2 tablespoons vegetable oil
1-1/2 cups fresh or frozen blueberries, optional

> Combine dry ingredients.
> Add egg, starter, milk and oil. Stir into the flour mixture just until well-mixed.
> Using two tablespoons batter for each pancake, bake on a hot, lightly-greased griddle until golden, turning once.

Makes about 28 pancakes

from **Hillside B&B**
Route 1-A, West Lakeshore Road
Cedar, Michigan 49621
616-228-6106

"Sourdough pancakes are usually served winter weekends -- in the summer, guests always seem to want to eat and run," said Innkeeper Jan Kerr. No wonder. This Victorian farmhouse has a hill to climb, a barn to explore and is located just minutes from swimming beaches, the picturesque fishing village of Leland, Sleeping Bear Dunes National Lakeshore, wineries, cherry orchards and all the attractions of Traverse City.

Jan and Don Kerr serve these pancakes with local berries, local maple syrup and local bacon to skiers who are staying in the two guest-rooms. "We like to provide hearty breakfasts before everyone leaves for a day of skiing," either alpine or cross-country. Coming back is a treat, too, since guests are warmed by the kitchen woodstove and welcomed by Victoria the dog and Albert the cat, in addition to their human hosts.

Another Hillside B&B recipe:
Sourdough Coffeecake and Starter, page 41

Cornmeal Belgian Waffles

Ingredients:

2 cups lukewarm milk
1 package dry yeast
4 eggs, separated
1 teaspoon vanilla
3-1/2 cups flour
1/4 cup plus 1 tablespoon sugar
1 teaspoon salt
1/2 cup butter, melted
3 cups cooked cornmeal

Cooked Cornmeal:
3 cups water
1/2 cup cornmeal
1/2 teaspoon salt

Also:

Fresh berries
Maple syrup

> To make cooked cornmeal, mix ingredients and boil gently over medium-low heat for 20 minutes. Allow it to cool to lukewarm.
> In a large bowl, stir milk, 1 tablespoon sugar and yeast until the yeast is dissolved.
> Add the vanilla and the beaten egg yolks.
> Stir in the flour, 1/4 cup sugar and salt.
> Mix in the melted butter, then the cooled cornmeal.
> Beat the egg whites until they form soft peaks. Fold them into the rest of the mixture.
> Allow the dough to rise in a warm place, covered lightly, for 60 to 90 minutes.
> Pour into a hot, seasoned Belgian waffle iron and bake. (If batter seems too runny, add a little more flour.)

Makes 6 servings

from **Triple L Farm**
Route 1, Box 141
Hendricks, Minnesota 56136
507-275-3740

These hearty waffles are served with plenty of maple syrup and fresh berries by Innkeeper Joan Larson. There's something about the country that makes guests hungry, and Joan and Lanny Larson have plenty of country to go around. They run a 283-acre farm, raising wheat, corn, beans and hogs in this southwestern Minnesota community.

Since opening in the summer of 1986, Joan has drawn upon her experience traveling in European B&Bs and working at the Trapp Family Lodge in Vermont. She wanted to share that kind of homey hospitality to guests who may never have been on a farm. The family has two guest-rooms available, with handmade quilts and antiques.

Gingerbread Waffles

Ingredients:

2 eggs
1/3 cup sugar
1/2 cup molasses
6 tablespoons shortening
1/2 cup hot water
2 cups flour
1 teaspoon ginger
1 teaspoon soda
1 teaspoon cinnamon
1/2 teaspoon salt

Also:

Apple cider sauce (see page 92), whipped cream and bananas or other topping

> Beat the eggs until they are lemon colored.
> Add the sugar and beat again. Add the molasses and beat again.
> Melt the shortening in the hot water.
> Add it to the egg mixture alternately with the sifted dry ingredients. Beat thoroughly.
> Bake on a hot waffle iron. Serve with whipped cream and bananas, apple cider sauce, warm applesauce, or lemon curd.

from **The Apple Orchard Inn**
Rural Route 3, Box 129
Missouri Valley, Iowa 51555
712-642-2418

Gingerbread waffles are a special Sunday morning brunch or dessert after a light lunch at this farmhouse inn, set amid an orchard and overlooking a valley "more beautiful than Ireland," said John Strub. Innkeeper Electa Strub might whip up a batch to serve lunch or dinner guests at the inn, in addition to her overnight guests.

She and John bought this historic farmhouse in 1987 and renovated from the plumbing up. Located on 26 acres, the old orchard needed some loving care, too, and John has planted hundreds of new apple trees and a few pear and plum trees. Guests find hiking trails amid the trees and have the use of the home's television and whirlpool. The three guest-rooms have 1930s decor.

Another Apple Orchard Inn recipe:
Apple Cider Sauce, page 92

Minnesota Wild Rice Waffles

Ingredients:

    3 eggs, separated
    1-1/2 cups milk
    1-3/4 cups flour, sifted
    4 teaspoons baking powder
    1/2 teaspoon salt
    1/4 pound margarine, melted
    1 cup or more cooked wild rice

> Beat the egg yolks with a fork or wire whisk.
> Stir in milk, flour, baking powder, salt and melted butter. Mix until smooth.
> Stir in the cooked wild rice.
> In a separate bowl, beat the egg whites until they form stiff peaks. Fold them into the batter.
> Bake in a hot waffle iron. Serve with maple syrup.

Makes 3 large waffles (12 quarters)

from **The Canterbury Inn**
723 Second Street SW
Rochester, Minnesota 55902
507-289-5553

"I just made it up -- I took a basic waffle recipe and added things that sounded right," said Innkeeper Mary Martin, who likes to do waffles more than partner Jeffrey Van Sant (she prefers, instead, to whip up a mean Eggs Benedict; see page 119). Mary describes this recipe as "different and pretty and elegant," but still remarkably easy.

These innkeepers are willing to do almost anything to make their guests' stay remarkably easy, too, including offering breakfast until noon and sometimes driving guests to appointments (with the Mayo Clinic and IBM in town, many guests are on business). The clinic, restaurants and shops are within a few blocks of this 1890 home.

Other Canterbury Inn recipes:
Pesto, page 97
Canterbury Eggs Benedict, page 119
Sourdough Crackers (Lavosch), page 212

Pecan Waffles

Ingredients:

3 eggs, separated
1-1/2 cups buttermilk
1 teaspoon baking powder
1/2 cup butter or margarine, melted
1 teaspoon baking soda
1 teaspoon vanilla
1 cup sour cream
1/4 cup sugar
1/2 cup pecans, chopped
2 cups flour

Also:

Maple syrup
Sausages
Apple cider

> Beat the egg whites until stiff. Set aside.
> In a large bowl, beat the remaining ingredients together.
> Fold in egg whites.
> Pour onto a hot waffle iron and bake.
> Serve with real, warm maple syrup and sausages steamed in apple cider and then browned.

Makes 10 waffles

from **Silver Creek B&B**
4361 U.S. Highway 23 South
Black River, Michigan 48721
517-471-2198

"Very rich," warns Innkeeper Kim Moses about these waffles, "but wonderful." Kim makes sure that other touches are added to breakfast here, like heating the plates and adding a teaspoon of cinnamon to the coffee pot. Served with fruit and homemade bread or rolls, this is an especially hearty breakfast with which to start off winter guests for a sleigh ride or sledding. Those wintertime activities are common in her neck of the woods in the northeastern Lower Peninsula.

Apple-Bacon-Cheddar Bake

Ingredients:

1/2 pound bacon, fried crisp and crumbled
About 1-1/2 cups apples, sliced
1 tablespoon sugar
1 cup cheddar cheese, shredded
1 cup flour
1-1/2 teaspoons baking powder
1/4 teaspoon salt
1 cup milk
3 eggs

> Mix flour, baking powder and salt.
> In a separate bowl, mix sliced apples and sugar. Place slices by rows in a 9 x 9-inch greased pan.
> Cover apples with cheese. Sprinkle with bacon.
> Beat remaining ingredients together.
> Using a ladle, pour the egg mixture evenly over the apples, cheese and bacon.
> Bake at 375 degrees for 25-35 minutes until lightly browned.

Makes 6 servings

from **The Griffin Inn**
11976 Mink River Road
Ellison Bay, Wisconsin 54210
414-854-4306

"This has been one of our most-requested recipes at the Inn," said Innkeeper Laurie Roberts. "Many guests report back that this has become their favorite entree when they re-create a Griffin Inn breakfast for *their* special guests!" The unexpected combination of baked fruit, meat, eggs and cheese is a mouthwatering surprise.

The Griffin Inn has been serving guests since 1921 when the brother and sister-in-law of the original builder opened the Ellison Bay Lodge. They added five rooms upstairs to the 1910 building and cottages out in back. It changed hands over the years and Laurie and Jim Roberts bought it in 1986.

Other Griffin Inn recipes:
Apple Squares, page 29
Old-Fashioned Oats Coffeecake, page 37
Orange Butter, page 96
Sesame Whole Wheat Pancakes, page 140

Bauernfruhstuck

Ingredients:

6 slices bacon, cut in small pieces
1/2 large green pepper, diced
1 tablespoon onion, finely chopped
1/2 cup cheese (not processed), grated
3 large boiled potatoes, peeled and cubed
6 eggs

Also:

Salt and pepper

> Fry bacon carefully until just browned lightly. Drain fat (leave 3 tablespoons if not using a non-stick pan).
> Add green pepper, onion and potatoes. Salt and pepper to taste.
> Cook over medium heat until potatoes are golden and hot.
> Break eggs into pan over potatoes, cook and stir constantly until eggs are set. (Eggs should coat the potatoes, not be in isolated chunks.)
> Toss in cheese. Turn and mix just until cheese begins to melt.

Makes 3-4 servings

from **Strawberry Hill B&B**
Route 1, Box 524-D
Green Lake, Wisconsin 54941
414-294-3450

This German farmer's breakfast is almost always on the menu as a specialty at Strawberry Hill. Innkeeper Patricia Spencer serves it with local pork sausage links and homemade sourdough biscuits on a hot plate.

Bauernfruhstuck (she gives lessons in pronunciation) is remarkably versatile. Preparations can be done the night before so the dish goes together quickly, she said. "While the proportions given here give a highly satisfactory dish, they are by no means written in stone. The home cook may increase, decrease or even omit without ruining the dish." Her only caution: "Give yourself a big enough pan to stir and toss comfortably." While Pat may cut up the ingredients ahead of time, everything in her kitchen is prepared fresh each morning, including hot breads.

Other Strawberry Hill recipes:
Strawberry Daiquiri, page 24
Christmas or Easter Danish, page 180

Individual Breakfast Strudel

Ingredients:

2 tablespoons butter
2 tablespoons flour
1 cup milk
8 tablespoons cheddar cheese, grated
2 tablespoons Parmesan cheese, grated
Pinch(es) of salt, cayenne pepper and nutmeg
1/4 pound bulk pork sausage
1/4 teaspoon thyme, powdered
1 tablespoon parsley, minced
5 eggs
Salt and pepper

Pastry:

8 fillo pastry sheets
1/2 cup butter, melted
8 tablespoons bread crumbs

> To make a white sauce, melt butter and stir in flour until smooth. Remove from heat. Add milk. Stir and boil for one minute until thick. Stir in cheeses, salt, cayenne and nutmeg.
> In a separate pan, cook the sausage, breaking it up with a fork.
> In a large bowl, mix eggs, thyme and salt and pepper. Add to the drained sausage and mix.
> Cook the egg-sausage mixture just until the eggs are set. Then add the white sauce and parsley. Cool completely.
> Unfold the fillo dough (note that it must be defrosted a day ahead of time). Cover with a damp cloth (follow directions on box for handling).
> Spread one sheet with melted butter. Sprinkle on 1 tablespoon dry bread crumbs and fold lengthwise in half. Brush the top of fillo with butter.
> Place 1/3-cup egg-sausage mixture at one end. Fold each side in 1/4-inch. Then fold end of the dough up to the mixture and roll it over and over (this will look like an egg roll).
> Brush with melted butter. Bake at 375 degrees for 15-17 minutes. (If storing before baking, wrap in plastic wrap and refrigerate.)

Makes 8 strudels

from **The Jefferson-Day House**
1109 Third Street
Hudson, Wisconsin 54016
715-386-7111

Innkeeper Sharon Miller finds this entree so popular that she doubles or triples the recipe. But breakfast in this 1857 home is a delight, no matter what's on the menu. Sharon and Wally Miller, their daughter and Wally's mother all assist in baking muffins, preparing fruit and serving the meal on antique dishes Wally and Sharon have collected.

Other Jefferson-Day House recipes:
Crepe Cups, page 150
Miniature Cheesecakes, page 178

Cooked Multi-Grain Cereal

Ingredients:
6 cups cracked wheat
6 cups old-fashioned rolled oats
6 cups coarse cornmeal
3 cups wheat bran, unprocessed or raw
3 cups brown rice
3 cups sunflower seeds, raw

Also:
1/4 cup raisins
1 apple, chopped
1 banana, sliced

> Mix dry ingredients and store in an airtight container. (This will keep several months in the freezer.)
> To serve, mix 1 cup dry mix to 3 cups hot water or milk. Mix well.
> Cover the saucepan and cook over low heat for 30 minutes.
> Add raisins, apple and banana, or a combination thereof, to the cereal during the last five minutes of cooking.
> Serve with cream and brown sugar, as you would oatmeal or other hot cereals.

from **Maggie's B&B**
2102 North Keebler Road
Collinsville, Illinois 62234
618-344-8283

Innkeeper Maggie Leyda says this healthy "stick-to-your-ribs" breakfast need only be accompanied by juice and coffee and perhaps hot bread or toast. This hot cereal is one of the choices she leaves for guests, who circle the items they'd like for breakfast the next morning. Other choices include biscuits and muffins made with stoneground flour, cheese grits, and toast from bread made with unbleached flour or whole wheat bread.

Maggie had toyed with the idea of being an innkeeper since a family trip to Europe years ago. In 1986, after a leisurely round-the-world cruise, she decided to give innkeeping a try as a "retirement business." The former boarding house and mine superintendent's home now draws guests from St. Louis who want a quiet getaway. Maggie urges her guests to try out the basement hot tub.

Another Maggie's B&B recipe:
Granola Banana Bread, page 71

Crepe Cups

Ingredients:

8 to 10 eggs
1/4 to 1/2 cup milk
1/2 teaspoon salt
1/4 teaspoon pepper
10 slices cooked bacon, crumbled
(or 1/2 pound cooked sausage or cubed, lean ham)
1/2 cup cheddar cheese, shredded

Also:

Sour cream

Crepes:
1-1/4 cups flour
2 tablespoons sugar
3 eggs
1-1/2 cups milk
2 tablespoons butter, melted
Up to 1 teaspoon lemon
     extract, optional

> To make the crepes, blend or mix all crepe ingredients well.
> Pour into five-inch circles on a well-greased skillet or crepe-maker and cook. (Makes about 24. Refrigerate extras or make all crepes ahead and store between waxed paper.)
> For the filling (fills about 12 crepes), mix all ingredients except the meat.
> Generously grease 12 muffin tins. Press cooled crepes into tins, being careful not to tear them while lightly ruffling the edges.
> Fill the bottom of tins with meat. Pour the egg mixture over the meat until the crepe cups are two-thirds full. Top with cheese.
> Put aluminum foil loosely over the crepe (so edges don't burn) and bake in a 350-degree oven for 15-20 minutes.
> Carefully remove the crepes from the tins with a spoon. Pass the sour cream for topping.

from **The Jefferson-Day House**
1109 Third Street
Hudson, Wisconsin 54016
715-386-7111

This recipe, with modifications, was passed along from a Colorado B&B. Guests at the Jefferson-Day House are served breakfast in the dining room, with a fire in the fireplace. During the three courses, innkeeper Wally Miller often leads the guests in "Know Your Dish," describing everything from Depression glass serving pieces to 1986 supermarket specials.

Wally and Sharon Miller, both teachers, joke that they had to buy this 1857 lumberman's home to house their antiques. They had to complete major restoration before opening in 1986, and the doorways still are wide enough for hoop skirts and the staircase remains worthy of a grand entrance.

Other Jefferson-Day House recipes:
Individual Breakfast Strudel, page 148
Miniature Cheesecakes, page 178

Elderberry Blossom Fritters

Ingredients:
 2 eggs
 1/2 cup milk
 2 tablespoons vegetable oil plus oil for frying
 1 cup flour
 1 teaspoon baking soda
 1/4 teaspoon salt
 6 large elderberry blossoms

Also:
 Sugar
 Favorite syrup, warm

> Mix the eggs, milk and oil. Add them to dry ingredients and beat with a mixer. Add a little more milk and oil if the batter seems too thick.
> Have the blossoms rinsed and dried (on a dish towel or paper towel).
> Pour oil into a skillet no deeper than one inch and heat to 375 degrees.
> "I usually break the blossom apart into fourths and make sure each fourth has a stem and dip it into the batter holding the stem."
> Fry the dipped blossoms until golden. Then drain on a paper towel.
> Sugar the hot fritters. Serve with warm syrup.

Makes 6 servings

from **The Farm Homestead**
W1982 Kiel Road, Route 2
New Holstein, Wisconsin 53061
414-782-5421

"When the elderberry blossoms are in full bloom -- usually mid-June -- find the blossoms along roadsides or fencelines. We just happen to have elderberry bushes in our backyard," said Innkeeper Marion Marsh. "The birds love the berries and are very possessive of the bushes. Birds may swoop down and try to prevent you from picking the blossoms. This is not a dangerous activity -- we consider this great fun. Use the blossoms shortly after picking and the fritters will have a wonderful elderberry flavor!"

At this farm house B&B, guests also can visit the dairy barn, have their lunch on the picnic table, or use the refrigerator. A homey country den with a fireplace is a popular gathering place, as is the large kitchen table.

Another Farm Homestead recipe:
Grandma's Iron Skillet Scrambled Eggs, page 122

Three Pepper Frittata

1/2 sweet red pepper
1/2 sweet green pepper
1/2 sweet yellow pepper
1 tablespoon butter
1/2 teaspoon garlic powder
1/2 cup caraway seed Monterey Jack cheese, grated
3/4 cup sharp cheddar cheese, grated
6 eggs
1 cup half-and-half

> Cut peppers into strips 1-inch wide. (Cut crosswise if peppers are longer than three inches.)
> Saute pepper strips in butter and garlic powder until heated through.
> Place strips into buttered individual ramekins or an 8 x 8-inch baking dish.
> Sprinkle cheeses on top of the peppers.
> In a small bowl, beat eggs and mix in half-and-half. Pour over the peppers and cheeses.
> Bake 30-35 minutes at 350 degrees. Serve immediately.

Makes 6-9 servings

from **Hannah Marie**
Country Inn
Route 1, Highway 71 South
Spencer, Iowa 51301
712-262-1286

"This dish will puff and become golden brown when it is ready to serve," said Innkeeper Mary Nichols, who likes to use fresh Iowa produce in her breakfasts. "This is as good as it smells."

This dish might be served with biscuits, fresh fruit and a dessert at the inn, which is in a restored, 11-room farmhouse that Mary and Ray, her husband, purchased in 1970. In 1983, they retired to the 200-acre farm from Southern California. In 1984, craftsmen from the Spencer area began renovation. The first guests arrived in 1986.

Breakfast might be served in the Good Morning Room, which has expansive windows looking out over the farm. Mary likes the windows in her kitchen, also. "I can look out and enjoy the fields and those Iowa blue skies."

Other Hannah Marie Country Inn recipes:
Mary's Elbows, page 26
Naughty Torte, page 209

Skillet Frittata

Ingredients:

1/3 pound sausage
1/2 cup onion, chopped
1/2 teaspoon dry mustard
1/4 teaspoon cumin
1/2 teaspoon thyme
1/2 teaspoon chili powder
3 small cooked potatoes, diced
3 eggs
1/3 pound favorite cheese, grated

> In a skillet, brown the sausage and the onion. Drain off the grease.
> Add the spices and potatoes.
> Beat the eggs and pour into sausage mixture. Cook until the eggs are firm. Stir to mix.
> Cover with grated cheese. Place under broiler to melt and brown the cheese.

Makes about 7 servings

from **The Gallery House**
215 North Main Street
Alma, Wisconsin 54610
608-685-4975

Innkeeper John Runions experimented until he perfected this recipe, which he heaps on plates at 8 a.m. It's no wonder that so many good spices are combined, since Joan, his wife, owns the Gallery Spice Shoppe on the first floor of this historic mercantile building. And the "Gallery" part comes from John, who is a watercolor artist and has Mississippi River views and steamboats among the art in his gallery, also on the street level.

This brick building has served Main Street in Alma since 1861. The first floor has been a general store, library, post office, hardware store, restaurant, antique shop and dentist office. Over the years, Alma thrived as a busy grain depot. Today, railroad tracks still run through town and a lock and dam on the river is just across the street. Upstairs, the former boarding house and apartments are now three guest-rooms. Guests enter the long hall from the back. The Runions' living and dining rooms are at the end of the hall. A deck goes around the side for guests' use.

Another Gallery House recipe:
Best-Ever Buttermilk Bran Muffins, page 47

Zucchini Frittata

Ingredients:

2 medium zucchini, grated
1 medium onion, finely chopped or grated
1 cup mozzarella cheese, shredded (save some for the top)
3 eggs, beaten
2 tablespoons flour
1 teaspoon basil
1 teaspoon oregano
Pinch of salt
Pinch of pepper

> Mix zucchini and onion together.
> Pan fry the mixture for five minutes in an oiled pan.
> Add the rest of the ingredients. Pour into a small casserole dish. Sprinkle a little mozzarella cheese on the top.
> Bake in a 350 degree oven for 30 minutes.
> Cut in squares or wedges and serve immediately.

from **The Renaissance Inn**
414 Maple Drive
Sister Bay, Wisconsin 54234
414-854-5107

This hearty vegetable dish is satisfying as an entree or may be used along with breakfast meats. JoDee Faller serves it along with meat, coffeecake, muffins and juices at this old-fashioned inn.

Located just a block from busy Highway 42 on a quiet residential street, the five guest-room inn is hidden from those who don't know where to go looking. It's also just a block from a municipal beach on Lake Michigan and from downtown shops.

Guests don't even have to go that far for lunch or dinner, since Faller's Seafood Restaurant is open downstairs in the summer (for dinner year 'round). John Faller put his 25 years as a chef to good use when they bought this place and moved to Door County to own and operate this small gourmet restaurant.

Other Renaissance Inn recipes:
Strawberry-Rhubarb Muffins, page 57
Zucchini Patties, page 173

Grandmother's Morning Treat

Ingredients:

Day-old homemade bread, cut in 1-inch slices
6 large eggs
1/8 teaspoon nutmeg
1/4 teaspoon cinnamon
1/4 teaspoon mace
1 teaspoon vanilla
3 cups cream from the top of milk pitcher
    (or 1-1/2 cups milk and 1-1/2 cups half-and-half)

Topping:
1/2 cup butter
1 cup brown sugar
2 tablespoons dark corn syrup
1 cup nuts, coarsely chopped

> Heavily butter a 9 x 9-inch baking dish. Fill the dish with bread slices so the bottom is completely covered and the dish is filled to the top.
> Mix the rest of the ingredients. Pour the mixture over the bread slices.
> Cover and refrigerate the dish overnight.
> In the morning, mix the topping ingredients (pecans, walnuts or hickory nuts are recommended).
> Spread the topping evenly over the bread slices.
> Bake at 350 degrees until puffed and golden, about 40 minutes.

Makes 4-6 servings

from **Just-N-Trails**
Route 1, Box 263
Sparta, Wisconsin 54656
608-269-4522

Innkeeper Donna Justin's grandmother used this recipe on her farm. "She made it in the evening and baked it after finishing chores in the barn in the morning, which is what I do for my guests," Donna said. Guests are welcome to watch the milking of about 30 cows from about 6:30 to 8 a.m.

Donna and Don decided to share the farmhouse in which Don grew up and opened their B&B in 1986 with two guest-rooms. They'd already opened a private cross-country ski touring center, as more than half their 200 acres are not tillable but great for x-c skiing and tubing. Their 25 kilometers of x-c trails are tracked and groomed and cut through forests and southwestern Wisconsin's limestone hills and valleys.

The home is decorated with family heirlooms. The four guest-rooms have three-foot grapevine wreaths made by Donna and designer linens. Summer guests eat breakfast on the back porch overlooking fields and woods.

Priznak

Ingredients:

1 package chopped frozen spinach, thawed and squeezed dry
1 pound American cheese, chunked
1 12-ounce carton cottage cheese
1/2 pound unsalted butter
6 eggs, lightly beaten
2 tablespoons flour

> Mix all ingredients in a greased two-quart casserole dish.
> Bake uncovered at 350 degrees for about one hour or until golden brown and bubbly.

Makes 4-6 servings

from **The Kirby House**
Center Street
at Blue Star Highway
Douglas, Michigan 49406
616-854-2904

Innkeepers Marsha and Loren Kontio derived this recipe from a gourmet club they belonged to several years ago, and today their guests enjoy this version of a Serbian spinach-cheese souffle. Guests serve themselves from a buffet maintained from early morning until early noon. They have several choices for seating, including the oak-paneled dining room, the country kitchen with wood cookstove, or, in summer, the 100-foot long wrap-around veranda or sun deck by the swimming pool.

The Kirby House is a century-old Victorian home built by Sarah Kirby, the daughter of a pioneer family of the area. Her family owned a local ginseng farm, exporting the roots to China, and, as a result, gained considerable wealth. The Kirby House stands on an acre of the original farm, located in Douglas, across the river from the Lake Michigan resort town of Saugatuck.

In 1984, the house was resurrected from unfortunate flophouse condition to its original beauty by 40 friends of the present owners. All eight guest-rooms have been furnished with antiques and some have fireplaces. Guests are welcome to start a fire in the foyer fireplace or to use the swimming pool, hot tub and barbeque grill.

River Run Sausage 'n Eggs on French Toast

Ingredients:

1 pound bulk country sausage
1 medium onion, chopped
1 5-ounce jar bacon-cheddar cheese spread
1/2 teaspoon garlic salt
1 clove garlic, finely chopped
2 tablespoons Worcestershire sauce
1 cup sour cream with chives
8 eggs
8 tablespoons milk
Strawberry jam, optional

For French Toast:
6 eggs
10 tablespoons milk
2 tablespoons vanilla
1/2 teaspoon salt
6 to 8 tablespoons margarine
4 sourdough English muffins

> For the sausage "topping," brown the sausage. Add the onion and cook until transparent.
> Mix in cheese spread, garlic salt, garlic and Worcestershire sauce over low heat. Then reduce heat to warm and keep warm until ready to use.
> For the French toast, beat the eggs and add the milk, vanilla and salt.
> Split muffins in half. Prick the muffins well with a fork before soaking for one minute each side in egg mixture.
> Fry the muffins on a griddle greased with margarine (or butter). Then keep in a warm oven until ready to use.
> Beat the 8 eggs and remaining milk and scramble the eggs.
> Top a slice of French toast with scrambled eggs (optional: spread jam over French toast first). Top the eggs with 2-3 teaspoons of the sausage mixture. Top the sausage mixture with a dollop of sour cream with chives.

Makes 8 servings

from **The Red Gables Inn**
403 North High Street
Lake City, Minnesota 55041
612-345-2605

"We wanted to do something different, something they would remember," said Innkeeper Bill Saunders. He was speaking about doing special brunches for groups at this Mississippi River town inn. Sourdough muffin French toast and eggs already were favorites of his guests when served separately. This recipe, as well as the brunches, have been a hit.

Other Red Gables Inn recipes:
BJ's Sticky Buns, page 85
Brown Cream and Fruit, page 107

Southern Grits and Sausage

Ingredients:

4 cups sharp cheddar cheese, shredded
4 eggs, beaten
1 cup milk
1/2 teaspoon dried whole thyme
1/8 teaspoon garlic powder
2 pounds mild bulk pork sausage, cooked, crumbled and drained

Cooked Grits:
2 cups water
1/2 teaspoon salt
1/2 cup uncooked quick grits

Also:

Tomato "roses" and parsley sprigs or sauteed or broiled tomato half

> To make the cooked grits, boil water and salt, stir in grits. Return to boil and reduce heat. Cook for four minutes, stirring occasionally.
> Combine cooked grits and cheese in a large bowl. Stir until cheese is melted.
> In a separate bowl, mix eggs, milk, thyme and garlic powder.
> Add grits mixture a little at a time to egg mixture and stir well.
> Mix in crumbled sausage and stir well.
> Pour the mixture into a 12 x 8-inch baking dish or ten 8-1/2-inch oblong ramekins.
> Cover and refrigerate overnight (or freeze ramekins not to be used the next day).
> Bake the large dish at 350 degrees for 55-60 minutes or ramekins for 20-25 minutes, or until the mixture bubbles. Garnish with tomatoes and parsley.

from **Bay Bed & Breakfast**
Route 1, Box 136A
Charlevoix, Michigan 49720
616-599-2570

Guests at Marian and Jackson Beatty's home feast on this sausage dish before, during and after being entranced with Lake Michigan from this contemporary and secluded lakeside home. The recipe is from a South Carolina B&B, but the atmosphere here is all Midwestern.

The Beattys turned their summer home into a year 'round residence in 1978 and opened two guest-rooms in 1984. Jackson was so busy with real estate business all summer that Marian was bored. "Fat chance to be bored now with the wonderful guests who share a love of the big lake with us!"

Located 12 miles south of Charlevoix and 40 miles north of Traverse City in a birch and hemlock grove, the home looks out over Lake Michigan and Grand Traverse Bay. Guests can beachcomb and hunt for Petoskey stones, swim or canoe on the lake. Others jog or walk the country lanes. From Charlevoix, travelers can take the ferry to explore Beaver Island. Fall colors and winter x-c and downhill skiing are popular in this area.

Trout Amandine

Ingredients:

8 to 10 ounce fresh, prepared trout per person
Salt and pepper
1/4 cup yellow cornmeal
1/4 cup flour

Sauce:
1/4 pound butter
Juice of 1/3 fresh lemon
1/3 cup sliced almonds

Also:

Vegetable oil for frying
Lemon slices and parsley sprigs

> Season the trout with salt and pepper.
> Mix cornmeal and flour. Roll the trout in it, being careful not to get the coating mixture inside the cavity of the trout.
> Heat oil 1/4-inch deep in a cast iron skillet.
> Brown the trout for three minutes on each side or until the flesh has turned from pink to opaque white.
> Melt butter, lemon juice and almonds together over low heat.
> Remove the trout and serve immediately with the sauce ladled over it. Garnish with lemon slices and parsley sprigs.

One trout serves one person

from **Seven Pines Lodge**
Lewis, Wisconsin 54851
715-653-2323

Trout for breakfast? "You bet," said Innkeeper Joan Simpson, whose Seven Pines Lodge has its own private, stocked trout stream. Some guests come to fish (no license, no limit) and have Joan cook their catch, but others enjoy the woods and let Joan worry about getting the fish out of the water. (She also will serve trout for dinner, by reservation.)

Charles Lewis, a wealthy Minneapolis stock broker and owner of a grain exchange, was the first to love the trout stream. He bought 1,530 acres from a St. Croix steamboat operator threatening to sell the virgin white pine to loggers. Lewis built a magnificent log estate in 1903, and today guests can stay in his lodge, stream house or gate house. President and Mrs. Calvin Coolidge once stayed in the lodge.

Other Seven Pines Lodge recipes:
Blue Trout, page 160
Joan's Lazy Cake, page 196

Blue Trout

Ingredients:

2 8 to 10 ounce fresh, prepared rainbow, brown or brook trout (with head left on)
Salt and pepper
Juice of 1 lemon OR 1/2 cup dry vermouth
6 carrot sticks
1 onion, coarsley sliced
Celery sprigs

> Season the trout with salt and pepper. Set aside.
> Prepare the poaching liquid in a special fish poacher, large-based kettle or frying pan.
Fill the container one-third full of water, or enough liquid to cover the trout.
> Add the lemon juice or vermouth, carrot sticks, sliced onion and celery sprigs. If lemon
juice is used, add the wedges after squeezing out the juice.
> Cover the container and bring the liquid to a boil.
> Carefully drop in the fish. Bring the liquid back to a boil, then turn off the heat, keeping
the pan covered.
> How do you know it's done? "The little eyeballs look like tiny white marbles." Let stand
five to 10 minutes. Serve with the carrot sticks and onions from the poaching liquid and
more fresh lemon wedges. Wild rice or boiled, parsleyed potatoes are good accompaniments.

Makes 2 servings

from **Seven Pines Lodge**
Lewis, Wisconsin 54851
715-653-2323

Innkeeper Joan Simpson will serve this trout recipe for breakfast by
request. Her breakfasts in the log dining room of the Lodge always include
homemade bread and jams, and the trout comes right out of the stream that
you can hear rushing by the lodge when the windows are open.

Seven Pines, which turned 85-years-old in 1988, is only 85 miles from
the Twin Cities. When Charles Lewis came up from Minneapolis to fish,
swim in his covered pool and entertain guests, he had to take the train. The
train once brought President and Mrs. Calvin Coolidge for an overnight at
the Lodge, en route to the Brule River in northern Wisconsin. The Coolidge
Room is still available for guests who wish to stay upstairs in the main
lodge, and many of Lewis' furnishings and memorabilia still remain.

Other Seven Pines Lodge recipes:
Trout Amandine, page 159
Joan's Lazy Cake, page 196

Be they side-dishes or garnishes, fruit, vegetable or cereal, sometimes it's what goes along with the main dish that sets a meal apart. Other times, there's no need for a main dish at all -- these dishes will suffice nicely alone. So here is an especially wide variety of dishes, from some basic recipes -- the kind mother never could write down because she just "knew" -- for Fried Tomatoes or Potato Pancakes, to more exotic fare, like Candied Violets or Lake Superior Trout Meuniere. (And anyone who's actually made maple syrup will agree it deserves to be considered a side-dish in its own right!)

Go-Alongs

John's Deviled Eggs

Ingredients:

12 eggs
1 tablespoon butter, softened
1 tablespoon hot sweet mustard with honey
1 teaspoon salad mustard
Dash celery salt
Dash pepper
1 tablespoon dried, minced onion flakes
1 tablespoon cider vinegar

Also:

Mayonnaise
Pimento-stuffed green olives, sliced
Paprika

> Boil the eggs until the yolks are hard. Cool and then peel the eggs and cut into halves.
> Put the egg yolks into a small mixing bowl and place the empty whites onto an egg serving plate. With a fork, crumble the yolks.
> Add the rest of the ingredients, plus enough mayonnaise to make a soft paste, and blend.
> Fill the "shells." Sprinkle the top with paprika and top with a slice of olive.

Makes 24

from **The Wisconsin House
Stagecoach Inn**
2105 East Main Street
Hazel Green, Wisconsin 53811
608-854-2233

Innkeeper John Mueller's deviled eggs often are on the antique, 16-foot dinner table on Friday and Saturday nights when he and Betha serve their by-reservation-only country inn suppers. Their suppers, which take all day to make for up to 20 people, feature recipes from inns around the country and include house wine and entertainment. The Mueller's brand of hospitality is something special here, as is the inn, itself. John says nothing in the inn (including the kitchen) is off-limits to guests. He and Betha have countless hours invested in this 1846 stagecoach stop, where Ulysses S. Grant often stayed when selling leather goods for his father's store in nearby Galena. All five guest-rooms and the rest of the inn are decorated with antiques and homemade country crafts and stenciled walls.

Another Wisconsin House Stagecoach Inn recipe:
Mom's Chili Sauce, page 94

Frau Paquin's Egg Roll-Ups

Ingredients:
>   4 eggs
>   4 tablespoons flour
>   4 tablespoons milk
>   Pinch of salt

Also:
>   Butter for frying
>   Chopped chives or green onion tops
>   Sugar

> Beat eggs, flour, milk and salt well. Flour must be blended in completely.
> In an 8-inch non-stick pan, melt 1 tablespoon butter for each roll-up.
> Just as the butter begins to sizzle and cover the whole pan, pour in about 1/4 cup batter.
> Just as the egg begins to set, flip the cake/crepe over. (If it breaks, put it back together with a spatula.)
> Again, just as the egg begins to set, roll up the crepe from one side, using a spatula and a table fork. Then remove to a small, heated platter.
> Sprinkle with chopped chives or green onion tops. "They become positively elegant if sprinkled with sugar and served with rolls and homemade jam."

Makes 4-6 roll-ups

from **Cedar Knoll Farm**
Route 2, Box 147
Good Thunder, Minnesota 56037
507-524-3813

"Frau Paquin was our German babysitter -- an elderly French woman," said Innkeeper Mavis Christensen, whose family spent three years as civilians in Germany. "She charmed our two oldest children into eating by fixing these in animal shapes and adding chopped apples as they cooked. The kids still ask for them when they are home, though they are now 28 and 30."

Mavis now serves them to guests at her Cedar Knoll Farm. The farmhouse is an 8-year-old Cape Cod charmer, decorated with antiques and treasures gathered during their residencies in Germany and Pennsylvania. Guests may want to join the family for popcorn around the fireplace or TV before retiring to one of three dormered guest-rooms, all with heirloom quilts.

Another Cedar Knoll Farm recipe:
Golden Fruit Cup, page 110

Lynn's Homemade Granola

Ingredients:

> 6 cups old-fashioned rolled oats
> 1/2 cup brown sugar
> 3/4 cup wheat germ
> 1/2 cup coconut
> 1/4 cup sesame seeds
> 1 cup nuts, coarsely chopped (pecans or walnuts work well)
> 1 cup raisins
> 2/3 cup honey
> 2/3 cup sesame oil
> 2 tablespoons water
> 1-1/2 teaspoons vanilla

> Mix the first seven ingredients.
> In a separate bowl, mix the honey, sesame oil, water and vanilla.
> Coat the dry ingredients with the honey mixture.
> Place the granola on a cookie sheet.
> Toast for 25-35 minutes in a 300-degree oven. Let cool thoroughly before storing in an air-tight container.

Makes 10 cups

from **The Greene House**
Rural Route 2, Box 214
Whitewater, Wisconsin 53190
414-495-8771

Innkeeper Lynn Greene finds this homemade granola is especially interesting to hikers, x-c skiers and bicyclists who stay at the Greene House while exploring the Southern Kettle Moraine State Forest's well-maintained trails. Breakfast is served about 9:30, but some eager beavers skip the big spread and enjoy this granola before hitting the trails as early as 6 a.m.

This five guest-room farmhouse, where Lynn was babysat as a child, allows Lynn and Mayner to combine all their interests and hobbies. He's a music teacher and has one room devoted to guitars. The barn is a gift and antique shop. Lynn runs her catering business from the home. The half-acre garden requires serious attention. And, having purchased the 1848 home for their B&B, house restoration has become a hobby, as well.

Another Greene House recipe:
Orange Cookies, page 186

Homemade Maple Syrup

Ingredients:

    200 gallons maple sap
    4 eggs
    2 cups fresh, whole milk

> "Sometime in March or April, depending on the weather -- it needs to be warm days and cold evenings -- we start by tapping maple sugar trees. We put out around 200 taps. Some trees might have two or three taps.

> "On these taps, we put gallon jugs or pails. When the sap is running well, we have to collect twice a day.

> "When we have around 200 gallons, we start cooking. We have a pit with a 60-gallon pan that sits on top. We cook this down until we only have about six gallons or a half-inch left. Then we bring it into the house to finish up.

> "I have two 16-quart pans I put this into, half in each, and add 2 eggs and 1 cup fresh milk to each pan. As it cooks, this purifies the syrup and brings the sand and other stuff to the top to be scooped off.

> "When the sap reaches 218 degrees, it is taken off and put through a wool cloth to make it nice and clear.

> "Then it is put into jars to be sold or used by ourselves."

Makes about 20 quarts

from **Lynch's Dream**
22177 80th Avenue
Evart, Michigan 49631
616-734-5989

Innkeeper Thelma Lynch claims there's no real recipe for maple syrup -- "It's mostly done by trial and error" -- but she came up with a pretty good account of what to do, should you have 75 or 80 sugar maples to tap, 200 taps in all. (By the way, don't stick your head over the boiling pots to inhale the scent because the syrup that's evaporating is in the steam and leaves a sticky residue!)

Those who can't or won't make it at home can have this homemade syrup on pancakes or waffles at Thelma and Dick's B&B. The Lynchs have a turn-of-the-century farm home with two guest-rooms, plus 37 acres to explore, near several good swimming and fishing lakes and the town of Big Rapids. "We got our B&B name as this was our dream for 20 years, to move back up here from Lansing," said Thelma. "I was born one-and-a-half miles from where we now live." At 18, she and her family moved to Lansing and she didn't move back until 1978.

Baked Stuffed Peaches

Ingredients:

    6 peach halves, preferably fresh
    1/2 cup sugar
    1/2 pound coconut macaroon cookies (about 1 small cookie per peach), crushed
    4 egg yolks

Also:

    Spiced rum (available at liquor stores)

> Scoop out 1 teaspoon of center pulp in each peach half.
> Mash the pulp with sugar, macaroon crumbs and egg yolks.
> In a greased glass pie plate or quiche pan, place the halves close together, cut side up.
> Spoon the macaroon mixture into the center of each peach. Drizzle each peach half with about 1 teaspoon of the spiced rum.
> Bake for 30 minutes in a 300-degree oven or until the peaches are tender.

Makes 6 servings

from **The Hutchinson House**
305 Northwest Second Street
Faribault, Minnesota 55021
507-332-7519

Innkeeper Marilyn Coughlin serves these hot peaches as a side dish when she serves seafood crepes or as a dessert for any breakfast that is "not too sticky-sweet."

Marilyn found that opening her B&B in this mansion, listed on the National Register of Historic Places, meant she could combine a number of loves and talents. She's always liked to cook, so she enjoys creating breakfasts that guests would not take the time to serve themselves at home. A former art teacher in Minneapolis, she's put her artistic skills to use painting a mural and redecorating this huge home. An antique collector of 25 years or more, she now has an historic home -- a treasure in itself -- that's big enough to house her smaller treasures. And, a former saleswoman for major corporations, she is putting her business skills to use, as well.

Other Hutchinson House recipes:
Celia's English Coconut Tea Loaf, page 73
Grandma's Custard Bread Pudding, page 197

Peach Meringues

Ingredients:

- 1 29-ounce can peach halves, drained
- 1/3 cup molasses or maple syrup
- 4 teaspoons butter
- 2 egg whites
- 1/4 cup sugar
- 1/2 cup heavy cream
- 1 tablespoon almond-flavored liqueur or bourbon
- Toasted almond slices, optional

> Place peach halves in a shallow baking pan.
> Top each half with 2 teaspoons of molasses and dot with 1/4 teaspoon butter.
> Bake at 450 degrees for 10 minutes
> Beat egg whites until stiff, but not dry. Add sugar gradually and beat until the sugar is dissolved or completely incorporated.
> Mound some of the meringue on each peach half.
> Mix liqueur and cream and pour around the peaches. Sprinkle tops with almonds.
> Bake five minutes longer, or until meringue is lightly browned.
> Serve peaches with the sauce in the pan.

Makes 4-6 servings

from **The Stout Trout B&B**
Route 1, Box 1630
Springbrook, Wisconsin 54875
715-466-2790

This recipe came from a friend when Innkeeper Kathleen Fredricks complained "there's nothing in the house" and she didn't want to make a winter trip 15 miles to Hayward for groceries. "I use it as a starter course for breakfast," she said. "This is a warm way to begin a winter's day."

People used to come to this country home on Gull Lake when it was a fishing resort or, in the 1920s, when it had a speakeasy. Now the intoxication comes from the comfortable surroundings and country air. Kathleen and Myke Carver opened the four guest-room B&B in 1987 after a year of extensive renovation. Today, the guest rooms have plank floors and antiques. Guests can dine or relax looking out over Gull Lake. Paddleboats, canoes and boats are ready at the dock, and x-c skiers can use the 40 acres.

Another Stout Trout recipe:
Kathy Cakes, page 136

Potato Pancakes

Ingredients:

- 1 pound russet or Idaho potatoes
- 1 medium onion
- 1 clove garlic
- 1 egg, slightly beaten
- 1/4 cup fine dry breadcrumbs
- 2 tablespoons flour
- 2 teaspoons baking powder
- 1 teaspoon salt
- 1/2 teaspoon pepper

Also:

Rendered chicken fat for frying (or vegetable oil, "but it won't be as good.")
Sour cream

> To render chicken fat (or it can be purchased rendered), cut the fat up into pieces, put it in cold water and bring the water to boil. Let it simmer until the water cooks out. When the fat is left, throw in a bunch of onions, a little garlic and potatoes. Simmer on low heat until vegetables are cooked crisp. Then strain and reserve the fat.
> For the potato pancakes, cut the onions, garlic and potatoes into chunks. Put in a food processor or blender with part of the egg for moisture and purée. Pour purée into a bowl.
> Combine the dry ingredients. Stir them into the purée.
> Heat a generous amount of chicken fat (or vegetable oil) in a heavy cast iron skillet. Spoon pancakes into the pan so they are silver dollar-size.
> Fry at medium heat for a few minutes, flipping when they look like they are drying out around the edges, and adding more fat/oil as necessary.
> Cook on the other side for five minutes or more, adding more fat or oil as needed.
> Serve with sour cream.

Makes 4-6 servings

from **The Collins House**
704 East Gorham Street
Madison, Wisconsin 53703
608-255-4230

Innkeeper Barb Pratzel grew up with these pancakes, often made by her father, an excellent cook. "We never had a recipe -- I do it by feel." Now, she serves them to guests as a side-dish to various egg dishes always on the Collins House menu on Sundays. Guests eat overlooking Lake Mendota.

Other Collins House recipes:
Raspberry Sauce Au Chambord, page 98
Pumpkin Pie, page 187

Rhubarb Fool

Ingredients:

2-1/2 cups young, fresh rhubarb, chunked
1/3 cup fresh-squeezed orange juice
1/2 teaspoon vanilla
3 tablespoons sugar
1 tablespoon butter
1/4 pint (1/2 cup) heavy cream
3 egg yolks

Also:

Whipped cream
Slices of orange peel and crystalized ginger

> Steam the rhubarb for five to 10 minutes, until tender but still firm.
> While the rhubarb is still warm, stir in the orange juice, vanilla, sugar and butter.
Let it cool and stand unstirred for 15 minutes.
> In a large saucepan, stir the cream and egg yolks over low heat until thickened into a custard. Cool.
> Mix the custard with the rhubarb mixture.
> Pour into parfait glasses. Top with whipped cream and decorate with slices of orange peel and crystalized ginger.

Makes 2 large servings

from **Barber House Inn**
410 West Mason Street
Polo, Illinois 61064
815-946-2607

Rhubarb is a prolific Midwestern vegetable, and the stalks from just one or two plants are more than one family usually can use in May and June when it's at its peak. Innkeeper Shirley Hinderaker takes advantage of its abundance and serves Polo House guests her creamy Rhubarb Fool.

Guests in this mansion most likely are awed by more than breakfast. Built in 1891 by Henry Barber, a prominent banker, the home is full of extraordinarily carved woodwork, plus hand-painted canvas-covered ceilings downstairs. The six guest-rooms upstairs have antiques or period reproductions and the original brass lighting fixtures.

Fried Tomatoes

Ingredients:

Ripe tomatoes, thickly sliced
1 cup flour
1 teaspoon sugar
1 teaspoon salt
4 tablespoons butter

White Sauce:
3 tablespoons flour
3 tablespoons butter
3 cups milk

> Dredge the tomato slices in a mixture of flour, sugar and salt.
> Heat butter in heavy skillet until it bubbles. Fry the tomato slices until they are golden brown and crisp on each side, adding more butter as needed.
> As you remove the slices, slip off the skins if they are loose. Keep the slices warm until all are browned.
> In the same skillet, make a thin white sauce. Brown slightly the butter and flour. Stir constantly so it doesn't scorch, and include all the pan scrapings.
> Remove from the heat and stir in 3 cups milk.
> Return to heat and stir until thickened. Test seasonings.
> Pour white sauce over hot tomato slices. Ladle into bowls to serve.

from **Greystone Farms B&B**
770 Adam's Church Road
East Troy, Wisconsin 53120
414-495-8485

Innkeeper Ruth Leibner said this recipe has been a family favorite for generations, and now she's glad to be sharing it with guests. "We like to serve it on a cool, early autumn day for a late Sunday brunch, when the garden is still yielding big red tomatoes." She called it "a special treat when served with thick slices of toasted homemade bread and butter."

Guests who rise early probably work up an appetite during a morning walk down a country road or fighting over whose turn it was on the tree swing. Guests can also hike, snowshoe and pick wild berries on the Leibner's 27 acres. Southern Kettle Moraine State Forest, with camping, mountain biking and x-c skiing, is only four miles away, as is Old World Wisconsin, an outdoor museum with restored historic buildings.

Other Greystone Farms recipes:
Danish Puff Cake, page 36
Spicy Tomato Jam, page 101
Overnight Pancake Batter, page 137

Lake Superior Trout Meuniere

Ingredients:

8 small fresh trout or 4 pounds fresh fillets
2 cups milk
1/2 to 3/4 cup flour
1 teaspoon salt
1/2 teaspoon black pepper, coarsely ground
1/2 teaspoon fresh dill
Vegetable oil
4 tablespoons butter

Also:

Lemon slices
Fresh parsley

> Clean the fish and rinse well under cold running water.
> Place the fish in a shallow pan. Cover with milk and let stand for 30 to 45 minutes.
> Remove from milk and drain, but do not dry.
> Mix salt, pepper and dill with flour. Coat fish one at a time in seasoned flour. Use additional flour as needed.
> Pour vegetable oil into a deep, heavy skillet to 1/2-inch deep. Heat on medium setting.
> Add trout when oil is hot and cook until golden brown on underside. Turn and brown again.
> Transfer fish to serving platter. Pour oil out of skillet and wipe dry with paper towels.
> Add butter to skillet and heat to sizzling. Pour butter over trout. Garnish with thin slices of lemon and fresh parsley sprigs.

Makes 8 servings

from **The Old Rittenhouse Inn**
Rittenhouse and Third
Bayfield, Wisconsin 54814
715-779-5111

"Several members of my staff were skeptical when I decided to offer trout as a side dish at breakfast," said Innkeeper Mary Phillips. But about a quarter of guests order it, fresh from Lake Superior two blocks away. Mary is in charge of the kitchen and her creations have been featured in "Gourmet" magazine. Guests at the Old Rittenhouse, Le Chateau Boutin and the Grey Oak Guest House gather at the main inn for breakfast and have a chance to talk with the innkeepers and staff about Bayfield attractions.

Other Old Rittenhouse Inn recipes:
Apple Cider Marmalade, page 91
Maple-Poached Pears, page 114

Candied Violets

Ingredients:

   1-1/2 cups sugar
   1/3 cup water
   1 cup violet flowers

> Boil sugar and water together until a candy thermometer registers 230 degrees.
> Add flowers and stir to combine completely.
> Bring syrup back up to 230 degrees.
> Pour mixture into lightly greased stainless steel bowls.
> Let the candied flowers harden.
> Place them in the sun or in a 200-degree oven to dry completely.
> Break into smaller pieces if desired.

from **Thorwood**
Fourth and Pine
Hastings, Minnesota 55033
612-437-3297

This "very seasonal" recipe, said Innkeeper Pam Thorsen, produces just beautiful garnishes for tarts and fruit plates. Thorwood guests might find the garnish on the evening snack tray, with local wine or catawba, fruit and pastries, after they return from dinner and head up to their room. Or they may find it in the morning when they are served breakfast, in their room, downstairs in the dining room or on the sitting porch, at the time they requested the night before.

Pam and Dick Thorsen specialize in catering to the wishes of the guests in their eight guest-rooms. Guests arrive to find their names on the door of their room, and each room is decorated with antiques. Some of the rooms have fireplaces and/or double whirlpool baths -- one has a steeple and another has a loft -- and Thorsens have worked hard to build up a clientele of honeymooners, anniversary couples and others looking for a romantic getaway. And every room has a teddy bear, carefully selected and placed by the Thorsens' two daughters.

Hastings is a Mississippi River town, and guests will find Lock and Dam #2 interesting to watch. They can also take a walking tour, tour a nearby winery and enjoy good food at Hastings restaurants.

Another Thorwood recipe:
Laurie's Poppy Seed Muffins, page 54

Zucchini Patties

Ingredients:

3 cups zucchini, coarsely grated
1 small onion, chopped
1 large egg
1/2 cup bread crumbs
1/2 teaspoon minced garlic
1/2 teaspoon cumin powder
1/2 teaspoon salt
1/4 teaspoon pepper
Fontina, Monterey Jack or Parmesan cheese, grated

> Mix all ingredients except the cheese. Pan fry the mixture in an oiled skillet.
> Top with grated cheese and serve.

Makes 4 servings

from **The Renaissance Inn**
414 Maple Drive
Sister Bay, Wisconsin 54234
414-854-5107

This is a super-simple side-dish that is healthy and hearty. Besides that, it's a way to use up some of those millions of zucchini that are silently overtaking Midwest gardens.

From the outside, this inn still looks like it could be a bait shop, an ice cream parlor, a grocery store, a stove store, a boarding house or a butcher shop. It has been all those things since being built in 1893. JoDee and John Faller put their seafood restaurant downstairs in the former storefront and porch. Their B&B is upstairs. The rooms are furnished with antique wood or iron beds and decorated with Renaissance art.

The boat docks, swimming beach, shops and art galleries are just a block away. A half-mile away is a golf course. Sister Bay is also close to two state parks: the large Peninsula State Park, with hundreds of camping spaces, a bike trail and beaches from which to watch the sunset, and Newport State Park, on the eastern side of Door Peninsula and blessed with secluded, sandy beaches and more primitive camping.

Other Renaissance Inn recipes:
Strawberry-Rhubarb Muffins, page 57
Zucchini Frittata, page 154

Anyone who has had to travel over a holiday, especially Christmas, can understand how it could be a depressing event. But holiday travel is done on purpose to many Midwest B&Bs. These wonderful old homes are decorated to the rafters with boughs and bows for Christmas. Another holiday that's even more popular at romantic inns is Valentine's Day, where lovers treat themselves to rooms with fireplaces, whirlpools or a four-poster bed. Whatever the holiday, innkeepers rise to the occasion with fantastic fare that now can be a family tradition at home, as well.

Holiday Fare

Christmas Scent

Ingredients:

- 4 cups water
- 1/2 of the peels from an orange
- 1/2 of the peels from a lemon or 2 tablespoons lemon juice
- 1 large cinnamon stick
- 6 cloves
- 1 bay leaf

> Combine all ingredients in a saucepan.
> Bring to a quick boil and then simmer for hours. Do not eat this, just enjoy the scent!

from **The Gables**
821 Dodge Street
Kewaunee, Wisconsin 54216
414-388-0220

If Christmas has a "smell," this is it. "Your house will smell so good!" guarantees Penny Dunbar, the Gables' innkeeper. "We started using this around Halloween through the New Year. It can be used in simmering pots throughout the home." Guests walk in and immediately feel relaxed and pampered, which is just what Penny and Earl Dunbar had hoped.

At the Gables, Penny and Earl want their guests to feel as much at home as they can in a 22-room historic mansion with handcrafted woodwork and glass. That is, of course, once the guests get inside. In the spring, that's a bit of a chore. They are out exploring the 500-daffodil garden Earl is restoring. This home, once owned by the daughter of the man who invented the pea harvester, had elaborate gardens, arbors and trellises that took up almost an entire city block. The Dunbars are using historic photographs to restore the gardens and look forward to hosting garden weddings.

Indoors, guests will be treated to wonders from the kitchen. Penny, who has contributed to microwave cookbooks and teaches classes on microwave cooking, believes strongly in featuring almost exclusively locally-made food. Guests enjoy locally-made fruit coolers and hors d'oeuvres upon arrival. Breakfast is served in the dining room overlooking the gardens. The four guest-rooms have antiques. Guests have use of a TV and game room and the living area.

Other Gables recipes:
Overnight Coffeecake, page 38
Breakfast Fruit Delight, page 183

Chokahlua Cheesecake

Ingredients:

Crust:
- 1/4 cup unsalted butter
- 1-1/3 cups chocolate wafer crumbs (27 wafers)
- 1 tablespoon sugar

Filling:
- 1-1/2 cups (9 oz) semisweet chocolate chips
- 2 tablespoons unsalted butter
- 1/4 cup chocolate-flavored liqueur
- 2 8-ounce packages cream cheese, softened
- 2 large eggs
- 1/3 cup sugar
- 1/4 teaspoon salt
- 1 cup sour cream

Topping:
- 1/4 cup semisweet chocolate chips
- 1 tablespoon chocolate liqueur
- 1 tablespoon light corn syrup
- 1 cup sour cream

> To prepare the crust: In a saucepan, melt butter. Remove it from the heat. Stir in wafer crumbs and sugar.
> Press into a 9 x 3-inch springform pan. Set aside.
> To prepare the filling: In a large saucepan, melt butter and chocolate chips and add liqueur. Stir constantly over low heat until smooth. Remove from heat.
> In a large bowl, beat the cream cheese until fluffly.
> Add the eggs, one at a time, and beat well.
> Add the sugar, salt and sour cream and beat well.
> Slowly beat in the slightly-cooled chocolate mixture.
> Pour filling onto the crust. Bake at 300 degrees for one hour or until center is barely set.
> Cool the cheesecake on a wire rack and then refrigerate at least three hours.
> To prepare the topping: Heat chocolate chips, liqueur and corn syrup over low heat, stirring until smooth.
> Remove and cool topping to room temperature.
> Remove sides of springform pan. Spread the sour cream on top.
> Drizzle the chocolate topping over the top, or pipe it into tree shapes or holiday decorations. (To make your own decorating bag from which to pipe the topping, take a sheet of waxed paper, make a triangular tube for a decorating bag, and fill with chocolate topping. Cut a small amount of the tip off and squeeze from the top.)
> Slice with a sharp knife dipped into cold water.
> Refrigerate unused portions.

from **The Westerfield House**
Rural Route 2, Box 34
Freeburg, Illinois 62243
618-539-5643

Holidays are a special time at the Westerfield House. This log cabin B&B and intimate gourmet dining establishment is decorated to the beams.

Marilyn Westerfield's Chokahlua Cheesecake is usually part of the Christmas menu, which changes every year to reflect the most popular dishes served during the past year. Marilyn pipes the chocolate topping over sour cream into outlines of pine trees whose trunks join in the middle. She believes that a chocolate treat is Christmasy, but this cheesecake is welcome year 'round.

Jim Westerfield closes up the place one weekend in November in order to prepare for their version of a Williamsburg Christmas. From mid-November to just after the New Year, visitors to this home, located a half-hour from St. Louis, are greeted on the porch by a barnwood sleigh.

Indoors, dark, cold winter nights are broken by the light of dozens of red candles and a crackling fire in the fieldstone fireplace. Red candles are hung in chandeliers over the tables and in candlesticks on the tables. The pineapple, a traditional symbol of hospitality, is used in centerpieces and decorations with red and green apples, pine boughs, holly and magnolia leaves. From beams, the aromatic result of the summer's extensive herb garden hangs amid red ribbons.

Marilyn and Jim are in their element. They want to create a Christmas fantasy for diners and overnight guests. The Westerfield House, they admit, has been a dream come true for them, "startlingly successful," Jim said.

He and Marilyn drew up an inventory of their skills and likes when, after 32 years in the grocery business, Jim soon was going to be out of a job. Marilyn had always loved gourmet cooking. They both collected antiques for three decades and share a keen interest in early American history. A B&B made sense. A year later, they added a 54-seat restaurant. Travel and food editors heard about the place, and publicity ensured their success.

Guests can choose from two guest-rooms. Jim gives them a complete tour of the home and grounds, including the herb garden. He built the log cabin himself in 1978, and then added a summer kitchen with a walk-in fireplace for authentic hearth cooking.

Another Westerfield House recipe:
Sweet Potato Muffins, page 59

Miniature Cheesecakes

Ingredients:

3 8-ounce packages cream cheese
1 cup sugar
5 eggs
1-1/2 teaspoons vanilla

Filling:

1 cup sour cream
1/2 cup sugar
1/4 teaspoon vanilla
1 21-ounce can cherry pie
filling

> With a mixer, combine cream cheese and sugar.
> Beat the eggs and add them to the cream cheese mixture. Stir in vanilla and whip.
> Pour into heart-shaped muffin tins until the tins are two-thirds full.
> Bake at 300 degrees for 40 minutes. Then remove from the oven and cool until there is a depression in the center.
> Mix the sour cream, sugar and vanilla. Spoon into the depression.
> Top with a small teaspoon of cherry pie filling. Return to oven for five more minutes.

Makes 2 dozen

from **The Jefferson-Day House**
1109 Third Street
Hudson, Wisconsin 54016
715-386-7111

This valentine treat can be made any time of the year, of course, using round muffin tins or another kind of pie filling or fruit. But at the Jefferson-Day House, holidays are special, and this large 1857 home is decorated for the season. Valentines have their choice of four upstairs guest-rooms, all decorated in antiques. The St. Croix Suite is a favorite of lovers and honeymooners, with an antique wedding dress on a dress form and a private sun porch on which breakfast may be served.

Guests are welcomed downstairs with appetizers in the living room, and they are invited to use the library with fireplace. Wally and Sharon Miller found this impressive home just a few blocks from the St. Croix River, where they enjoy boating, and in 1986 it became Hudson's first B&B. Wally's mother, Marjorie, operates it during the week. Sharon and Wally are both teachers, and they put on their innkeepers' hats on weekends and in the summer. Guests are encouraged to explore the river town or to boat, bike and ski.

Other Jefferson-Day House recipes:
Individual Breakfast Strudel, page 148
Crepe Cups, page 150

Strawberry Cheddar Cheesecake

Ingredients:

1-1/2 cups graham cracker or vanilla wafer crumbs
2 tablespoons butter, melted
2 8-ounce packages cream cheese, softened
1/2 cup sharp cheddar cheese, shredded
3/4 cup sugar
3 eggs
1 teaspoon orange juice or grated peel
1 teaspoon lemon juice or grated peel
2 tablespoons flour
1 cup whipping cream
1 pint fresh strawberries (or cherry pie filling or other pie filling)

Also:

Light corn syrup

> Mix the crumbs with butter. Press over the bottom of a 9-inch springform pan.
> Bake in 350-degree oven for five minutes.
> While crust is baking, beat the cheeses and sugar together until fluffy. Then beat in eggs.
> Add juices or peels, flour and 1/2 cup cream.
> Pour over the crumb crust. Bake at 350 degrees for 40 minutes or until set in the center.
> Remove from the oven and cool. Arrange whole strawberries on top of the cheesecake. Brush them with corn syrup.
> Whip the remaining cream and pipe a border around the strawberries. Keep refrigerated.

from **Evergreen Knoll Acres**
Country Bed & Breakfast
Rural Route 1, Box 145
Lake City, Minnesota 55041
612-345-2257

"Being a dairy farmer, I try to use dairy products. Strawberry Cheddar Cheesecake is a good example," said Innkeeper Bev Meyer. If strawberries are out-of-season, a canned pie filling can be used for the topping instead. Bev serves this cheesecake on Valentine's Day weekend. "This year I used cherry pie filling on top and swirled a few hearts in the center with the glaze from the pie filling." In 1986, Bev and Paul opened their home on a working dairy farm to guests who choose from three guest-rooms.

Other Evergreen Knoll Acres recipes:
Streusel Coffeecake, page 42
Aunt Clara's Strawberry Jam, page 99
Fresh Fruit Pizza, page 205

Christmas or Easter Danish

Ingredients:

3-1/2 to 4 cups unsifted flour
1/2 cup sugar
1-1/2 teaspoon salt
2 tablespoons cornstarch
1-1/2 teaspoon lemon peel, grated
2 packages dry yeast
3/4 cup milk
1/2 cup water
1/4 cup butter
2 eggs at room temperature, to be separated
1-1/2 cups butter, very cold
1 tablespoon water

Also:

Powdered sugar frosting
Colored sugar sprinkles

> In a large mixer bowl, mix thoroughly 1-1/4 cups flour, sugar, salt, cornstarch, lemon peel and undissolved yeast.
> Combine milk, water and 1/4 cup butter in saucepan. Heat until liquids are warm (butter doesn't need to melt), close to 115 degrees for the next step.
> Have mixer running and pour milk mixture slowly into flour mixture. Beat two minutes at medium speed, scraping bowl.
> Add 2 egg yolks, 1 egg white and about 3/4 cup flour to make a thick batter. Beat at least two minutes ("longer doesn't hurt") at high speed, scraping the bowl.
> Remove beaters and add enough flour to make a stiff batter. Stir just until blended.
> Cover tightly. Chill about an hour.
> While chilling: on waxed paper, spread 1-1/2 cups butter into 10 x 12-inch rectangle. (This is easily done by slicing thin slices with a wire cheese slicer.)
> Cover with waxed paper and roll to blend pieces. Return to refrigerator and chill 1 hour.
> On a lightly floured board, roll chilled dough into a 12 x 16-inch rectangle.
> Place butter sheet over two-thirds of dough and remove waxed paper. Turn unbuttered end toward the middle, fold the opposite end (buttered) over the center. (You will have dough, butter, dough, butter, dough). After folding in each end, give dough a quarter turn; roll into a 12 x 16-inch rectangle. Fold in thirds from each end as above.
> Give a quarter turn and repeat two more times. You must work quickly and the cooler the kitchen, the better.
> Wrap loosely and refrigerate for at least one hour.
> Repeat procedure of two rollings, foldings, turnings and chillings two more times. Then refrigerate overnight.

Day 2:

> Roll half the dough into a 15 x 6-inch rectangle.
> Cut 12 strips 15 inches long and 1/2-inch wide.
> Hold the end of each and twist gently. Form into circle on a lightly-greased baking sheet.
> Seal ends by pinching. Cover loosely with plastic wrap and refrigerate overnight again.
> Repeat with the second half of the dough.

Day 3:
> Combine 1 reserved egg white with 1 tablespoon water. Brush rolls with mixture.
> Bake in 375-degree oven about 15-20 minutes. Watch closely so the rolls only color slightly. Remove and cool on wire racks.
> Frost with powdered sugar frosting and decorate with colored sprinkles.

from **Strawberry Hill B&B**
Route 1, Box 524-D
Green Lake, Wisconsin 54941
414-294-3450

Actually, this is not as difficult as it appears, said Innkeeper Patricia Spencer, who doesn't want the long list of directions to discourage cooks.

"These are a three-day project, but have long been a family tradition, served to my family at Christmas and Easter, without which neither holiday would have been complete. My guests have enjoyed them equally."

Patricia times her baking "so guests may enjoy the tantalizing fragrance as well as the delicate texture." The aroma of Danish baking and the taste of fresh-baked is much better than reheated, she believes. The dough will keep in the refrigerator an extra night at any part of the process, "so bake only what you will use at one sitting." Another tip is to freeze leftovers, since they do freeze well, but reheat them for only a few minutes in an oven -- not in a microwave, she cautions.

Not every Strawberry Hill guest is lucky enough to have the smell of fresh holiday Danish wafting upstairs to the guest-room. But all are greeted with a strawberry daiquiri and Patricia's hospitality. Her breakfasts include coffee made with excellent well water. No mixes and only natural dairy products are used in preparing breakfast. Almost all of the fruits and vegetables served come from the farm. Cloth napkins and table linens grace the dining room table or the table on the solar porch.

After breakfast, guests might take a bike ride on the country roads or head for Green Lake's shops and beach, two miles away. Canoeing is within a half-mile and there are three golf courses within six miles.

Other Strawberry Hill recipes:
Strawberry Daiquiri, page 24
Bauernfruhstuck, page 147

Christmas Cranberry Wine

Ingredients:

3 cups cranberries, chopped
3 cups sugar
2 bottles Sauvignon blanc wine

> Chop the cranberries, fresh or frozen, in a food processor.
> Mix in sugar, then wine.
> Set aside and marinate for 22 days. Shake occasionally during the process.
> Strain before serving. Serve chilled or on ice.

from **The Victorian Swan
on Water**
1716 Water Street
Stevens Point, Wisconsin 54481
715-345-0595

"I start this wine after Thanksgiving to have it ready to serve Christmas guests," said Innkeeper Joan Ouellette. "The cranberries are great over ice cream, used as garnish for fresh fruit dishes or in breads and muffins."

Cooking is no chore for Joan, who has always worked in service jobs. It didn't surprise her brother, Chuck Egle, when she said she wanted to open a B&B. He knew about this historic home being for sale and he helped her buy it, get the zoning approval, and do the restoration. Guests can see photos of some of the stripping and other restoration work. It was started by a previous owner, but the bulk of the work fell on their shoulders.

In the process, some beautiful original light fixtures, for instance, have been saved. The living room has a black cherry fireplace, which works and is available for use by guests. The living and dining rooms still have heavy sliding doors, which work well today for business meetings or parties.

Guests here are only a few blocks away from public areas along the Wisconsin River, where they can x-c ski or skate. In the summer, Joan will pack a breakfast basket for those who want to picnic by the river.

Another Victorian Swan recipe:
Pecan Stuffed French Toast, page 129

Breakfast Fruit Delight

Ingredients:

    1 8-ounce package cream cheese, softened
    2 cups sour cream
    1 tablespoon sugar
    Favorite fresh fruit

> Prepare the first three ingredients the night before. Blend them until smooth.
> Place in one large mold or several individual molds -- such as heart-shaped for
Valentine's Day -- lined with cheesecloth to prevent sticking.
> Refrigerate overnight.
> When it's time to serve, turn out the molds onto serving dishes (or, using a small scoop,
scoop a portion onto serving dish).
> Surround the mold with fruit.

from **The Gables**
821 Dodge Street
Kewaunee, Wisconsin 54216
414-388-0220

With strawberries and heart-shaped molds, this sweet red-and-white side
dish is perfect for Valentine's Day at the Gables. (The romantic weekend at
this Queen Anne mansion includes a sleighride with a bonfire.) Penny
Dunbar also says she likes this recipe with a mixture of strawberries,
green grapes, bananas and peach slices, or other fresh fruit in season.

Every day of the year should be a holiday here. The Gables B&B is a lovely
old mansion which Penny and Earl are restoring, and that's worth
celebrating. Once one of Kewaunee's grandest homes, it was overgrown and
neglected when they purchased it. But many of the original light fixtures,
wallpaper and tile remained in good shape. The original leaded glass
windows and unusual glass block walls in the kitchen are exquisite.

Kewaunee is worth celebrating, too. The Gables is located just three blocks
from Lake Michigan, where guests can swim or beachcomb in the summer
and marvel at the changing lake any day of the year. The car ferry to
Michigan docks here. Kewaunee also has a jail museum, a lighthouse, local
artists' shops and plenty of outdoor recreation worth exploring.

Other Gables recipes:
Overnight Coffeecake, page 38
Christmas Scent, page 175

Irish Soda Bread

Ingredients:

2 cups flour
1-1/2 teaspoons baking powder
3/4 teaspoon salt
3 tablespoons sugar
1-1/2 teaspoons caraway seeds
3 tablespoons shortening
1 cup buttermilk
2/3 cup raisins, coarsely chopped

Also:

Butter, melted
Sugar

> In a large bowl, sift the flour with other dry ingredients. Then add caraway seeds.
> Cut in shortening with a pastry blender or fork until the mixture is in fine pieces.
> Make a "well" in the center of the dough. Pour in the buttermilk.
> Add raisins. Mix lightly to a moderately-soft dough.
> Turn the dough out onto a floured board. Knead gently for a few strokes.
> Shape the dough into a round. Place it into a greased 8 or 9-inch round layer cake pan.
> Cut loaf crosswise into quarters about two-thirds through the dough, using a sharp knife or scissors.
> Brush the top with melted butter and sprinkle with additional sugar.
> Bake at 350 degrees for about 30 minutes.

Makes 6-8 servings

from **Noni's B&B**
516 West Main Street
Warren, Illinois 61087
815-745-2045

This rich, yeast-less bread is always a hit, especially on St. Patrick's Day and especially straight out of the oven, said Innkeeper Naomi McCool, who is often called "Noni" by friends who can't pronouce or spell her name. "My late husband was Irish and he loved the Irish Soda Bread. It became a family favorite and a tradition for St. Patrick's Day."

Noni's B&B has two guest-rooms and is four blocks from Warren's business district. It's within walking distance of Meridian Park, located on the 90th principal meridian, where visitors can play tennis, swim or picnic. The home is decorated with traditional furniture from the 1940s and antiques.

Another Noni's B&B recipe:
Zucchini Pineapple Muffins, page 60

Norwegian Puff

Ingredients:

2 cups flour
1 cup butter
1 cup plus 3 tablespoons water
3 eggs
1-1/2 teaspoons vanilla

Frosting:
1 cup powdered sugar
1 tablespoon heavy cream
1/2 teaspoon almond extract
1 tablespoon butter

Also:

Red and/or green maraschino cherries or food coloring

> To make the bottom layer, mix 1 cup flour and 1/2 cup butter as for a pie crust, with a pastry blender or fork. Add 3 tablespoons water as needed.
> Spread the blended mixture on a round 18-inch ungreased pizza pan or baking sheet.
> Place the remaining butter and water in a sauce pan. Heat to boiling.
> Remove from heat and add the remaining flour.
> Beat the mixture until smooth. Cool slightly.
> Add the eggs, one at a time, beating well after each addition. Beat in vanilla.
> Spread this mixture lightly over the bottom layer.
> Bake for 40 minutes at 375 degrees. Then reduce heat to 300 and bake for 20 minutes.
> For the frosting, beat all ingredients well with a mixer. Spread over cooled puff and decorate with red or green cherries, depending on the holiday, or add food coloring to frosting.

Makes 12-15 servings

from **The Montgomery Mansion B&B**
812 Maple Avenue
Decorah, Iowa 52101
319-382-5088

When Christmas, Valentine's Day, Washington's Birthday or St. Patrick's Day roll around, Innkeeper Diane Ward gets the appropriately colored cherries and whips up a Norwegian Puff. "It is a great pastry for breakfast or brunch," she said. "The recipe is from a neighbor of mine who was famous for her puff. Everyone likes it as it just melts in your mouth."

A Norwegian recipe is appropriate from Decorah, as it is home to the American-Norwegian Museum and is called the immigrants' gateway to the north and west. Diane and Bob Ward have opened four guest-rooms in this 1800s brick home, located on three city lots. A library and screened porch are open to guests.

Orange Cookies

Ingredients:

2 cups unsalted butter, softened
1-1/3 cup sugar
2 egg yolks, slightly beaten
1 teaspoon vanilla extract
1 teaspoon orange extract
4 cups flour
2 tablespoons orange rind, grated
1 teaspoon orange food coloring

For "Rind" Dough:
Half of all ingredients
(except no orange rind or
orange food coloring)

> Two batches of dough are made: the orange batch is the inside of the cookie; the plain batch becomes the orange "rind."
> To make each batch, cream the butter. Add sugar and egg yolk and mix until light and creamy. Add the extracts, grated rind and coloring and mix again. Add flour gradually.
> Take the orange dough and roll it out into a long tube shape (like clay) about 1-1/2 inches in diameter. Set aside.
> Take the plain dough and roll out a rectangular shape as long as the tube and wide enough to wrap around it. Then place the orange tube on top and roll up the plain dough around it.
> Wrap well with plastic wrap. Freeze dough for at least two hours.
> Slice off cookies 1/4-inch thick and place on an ungreased cookie sheet.
> Using a butter knife, lightly mark lines resembling segments found in real oranges.
> Bake at 350 degrees for 10-12 minutes.

Makes 4 dozen

from **The Greene House**
Rural Route 2, Box 214
Whitewater, Wisconsin 53190
414-495-8771

"Every year, just in time for Christmas gift-giving, my mom and all the sisters would gather in the kitchen, put all the leaves in the table and make cookies and cookies and even more cookies," said Lynn Greene. "In re-living these memories, I found a way to work these little buttery treats into the breakfast I now serve to our visiting guests: make them look like oranges!" The cookie-marathons were good training for her innkeeping and catering business she runs out of the century-old farmhouse that's now a B&B.

Another Greene House recipe:
Lynn's Homemade Granola, page 164

Pumpkin Pie

Ingredients:

1 tablespoon unflavored gelatin
1/4 cup water
3 eggs, separated
1/2 cup brown sugar
1-1/4 cups canned pumpkin
1/2 cup milk
1/4 salt
1/2 teaspoon nutmeg
1/2 teaspoon cinnamon
3/4 cup sugar
1 tablespoon cognac

Gingersnap Crust:
22-25 gingersnap cookies
(1-1/2 cup cookie crumbs)
3 tablespoons butter, melted
3 tablespoons sugar

Whipped Cream topping:
1 cup whipping cream
1 teaspoon sugar
1 tablespoon cognac
Cinnamon

> For the crust, combine ingredients and press into a 10-inch pie pan. Bake for five minutes at 350 degrees and cool thoroughly.
> For the filling, mix the 3 egg yolks, brown sugar, pumpkin, milk, salt, cinnamon and nutmeg in the top of a double boiler. Stir and cook until thick. Remove from heat.
> Dissolve gelatin in the water. Add the gelatin/water mixture. Cool until set.
> Whip the egg whites with the cognac until stiff but not dry. Fold into the cooled pumpkin mixture.
> Stir in the sugar. Pour the filling into the crust. Refrigerate several hours or overnight before serving.
> Whip the cream with sugar and cognac. Dollop on top of the pie. Sprinkle with cinnamon.

from **The Collins House**
704 East Gorham Street
Madison, Wisconsin 53703
608-255-4230

"When this pie recipe was introduced to our family, there was never any other pumpkin pie we ate," said Innkeeper Barb Pratzel. "It's light and it's not baked and has gelatin, which gives it a whole different consistency."

Barb was raised in a gourmet cooking family and her father was teaching her cooking at the age of 3. "I always knew in the back of my mind I wanted to do something professionally with cooking, someday, somehow." After she and husband Mike started the B&B, a catering business followed naturally.

Other Collins House recipes:
Raspberry Sauce Au Chambord, page 98
Potato Pancakes, page 168

Raspberry Champagne Punch

Ingredients:

    750 ml (approximately 1 quart) dry white wine, chilled
    750 ml Champagne, chilled
    750 ml white soda, chilled
    2 shots raspberry-flavored liqueur
    1 pint fresh or frozen raspberries

Also:

    Red and green maraschino cherries

> Combine all ingredients except cherries in a punch bowl just prior to serving.
> Make an Ice Christmas Wreath by freezing cherries in a bundt pan (or gelatin mold). Float it on top of the punch just before serving.

Serves 10-12 guests

from **The Quill and Quilt**
615 West Hoffman Street
Cannon Falls, Minnesota 55009
507-263-5507

This special punch looks very Christmasy with the floating raspberries and the ice wreath Innkeeper David Karpinski uses to top it off. Guests report the punch is extra-tasty when sipped by the fresh, 10-foot Christmas tree done up in the front parlor.

The rest of the Quill and Quilt B&B looks very Christmasy, too, with lights, greenery and ornaments decorating it from top to bottom. Christmas is a specialty here. Guests can sit down to a traditional Christmas dinner with all the trimmings, from David's homemade oyster stew to co-innkeeper Denise Anderson's wild rice soup for starters all the way to pumpkin pie.

Denise and David opened this 1897 Colonial Revival home in 1987. Four guest-rooms have been furnished with antiques and Denise's handmade quilts. Her quilts, along with those made by her great-grandmother, gave the inn half its name; the other half is due to David's writing.

Other Quill and Quilt recipes:
Frozen Blueberry Muffins, page 49
Banana Bread, page 70
Basic Quiche Lorraine, page 123

Special Valentine Meringues

Ingredients:

 4 egg whites
 1-1/4 cup sugar
 Pinch of salt
 1/4 teaspoon cream of tartar
 1 teaspoon white vanilla flavoring (Watkins), optional
 Red food coloring - a drop or two to make pink tint
 6 ounces semisweet chocolate
 3 tablespoons water
 1 cup heavy cream
 1 pint fresh strawberries

> Beat the egg whites, salt, cream of tartar, vanilla and red food coloring until frothy. Add 1 cup sugar a little at a time.
> Cut a heart pattern from a four-inch square of paper. Cover a baking sheet with waxed paper. Trace eight hearts, using the heart pattern, spacing one inch apart (do not cut out).
> Spread the meringue 1/4-inch thick over each traced heart shape.
> Bake the hearts at 275 degrees for one hour. Then turn off the oven and let them dry in the closed oven for another hour. Cool thoroughly.
> In a double boiler, melt the chocolate and water.
> Whip 1 cup cream with 1/4 cup sugar.
> Slice the strawberries, saving eight pretty ones for garnish.
> Two to three hours before serving, spread each meringue with a thin coat of chocolate.
> Top with sliced strawberries, then with whipped cream (may use a pastry tube to spread).
> Garnish with the remaining strawberries, sliced through the center but kept intact with the stem attached. Lay each strawberry flat on top of the whipped cream.
> Drizzle chocolate over the top.

from **Bluff Creek Inn**
1161 Bluff Creek Drive
Chaska, Minnesota 55318
612-445-2735

Valentine's Day is cause for special celebration here, and Innkeeper Anne Karels adds these pink heart-shaped meringues to the breakfast menu. Not only are they pretty, but the decadence of chocolate and whipped cream, plus the treat of fresh strawberries in February, makes her Valentine guests feel absolutely sinful.

Other Bluff Creek Inn recipes:
Candlelight Coffee for Two, page 22
Stuffed Baked Apples, page 103

Wassail

Ingredients:
5 quarts apple cider
2 cinnamon sticks
1 teaspoon nutmeg
1/2 cup honey
1/3 cup lemon juice
2 teaspoons lemon rind, grated
2 46-ounce cans pineapple juice

Also:
Orange slices
Whole cloves

> Add cinnamon sticks and nutmeg to the apple cider. Heat the mixture to boiling and then simmer it for five minutes.
> Add the remaining ingredients. Simmer for 15 minutes more.
> Before serving, garnish the mugs using orange slices studded with whole cloves (stick the cloves into the whole orange, then slice).

from **The Parkside**
402 East North Street
Appleton, Wisconsin 54911
414-733-0200

Innkeeper Bonnie Riley described this holiday treat as "a nice, warming juice-type wassail, appropriate for breakfast." It's also appropriate for holiday parties, a toast on New Year's Eve, and to warm-up carolers, skaters or skiers. The aroma is nearly as comforting as the drink itself.

Surely holidays in this neighborhood were memorable. Harry Houdini and Edna Ferber each lived near this home, which was occupied until 1961 by one family, the founders of Geenan's Department Store in downtown Appleton, just a few blocks away. The three Geenan sisters lived here, then deeded it to a niece. During World War II, an apartment was added so that Geenan "children" who married had a place to live while getting started. That renovated apartment is now the B&B. The suite has a bedroom, living room, kitchen, bath and a reading nook, which overlooks the park.

Other Parkside recipes:
Applesauce Biscuits, page 64
Baking Powder Biscuits, page 66

Who was it, anyway, who decided that dessert should be reserved for after luncheons or dinners? And why did we ever listen to that person? A number of sensible innkeepers have ignored this ridiculous "rule" and are serving dessert after breakfast. Seven sweet treats are included here. Please note that at least twice as many recipes in other categories would work well as dessert for breakfast, though the innkeepers are not now serving them as such. (We can only hope that changes soon!) Consider this a challenge to add dessert to your next brunch!

Dessert for Breakfast

Hot Apple Crisp

Ingredients:

    6 cups apples (Cortlands, Jonathans or MacIntosh), peeled and sliced
    1/3 cup flour
    1 cup old-fashioned rolled oats
    1/2 cup brown sugar
    1/2 teaspoon salt
    1 teaspoon cinnamon
    1/3 cup butter, melted

> Place apple slices in a buttered 9 x 13-inch baking dish.
> Combine the dry ingredients. Add melted butter. Mix until crumbly.
> Sprinkle on top of apples.
> Bake at 375 degrees for 30 minutes or until apples are tender.
> Serve with yogurt, whipped cream or ice cream on top, if desired.

Makes 6-8 servings

from **The Inn at**
Cedar Crossing
336 Louisiana Street
Sturgeon Bay, Wisconsin 54235
414-743-4200

Apple Crisp is often considered a dessert, but it's a perfect way to start a crisp fall or winter day in Door County and that's why guests will often find it among the homemade breakfast offerings at this country inn.

It's a good thing breakfast is offered until 10 a.m. here, because there are some spectacular beds in this inn that are difficult to crawl out of. A huge pine poster bed in the Lilac Room was made for the inn by a Sturgeon Bay craftsman. Also custom-crafted is an oak cannonball bed in a suite. In a traditional-style guest room there's a bonnet-top maple pencil poster bed with a hand-tied canopy. There's also a brass canopy bed and an antique iron bed trimmed in a Laura Ashley comforter and dust ruffle.

Other Inn at Cedar Crossing recipes:
Apple Yogurt Coffeecake, page 30
Surpise Muffins, page 58
Fresh Rhubarb Bread, page 84
Zucchini Chocolate Nut Bread, page 88
Nectarines with Cream Anglaise, page 113
Crispy Caramel Corn, page 202

Chunky Apple-Pecan Cake

Ingredients:

- 3 cups flour
- 2 teaspoons cinnamon
- 1 teaspoon baking soda
- 1 teaspoon salt
- 1 cup vegetable oil
- 1/2 cup unsalted butter, melted
- 2 cups dark brown sugar, firmly packed
- 3 large eggs
- 2 teaspoons vanilla
- 3 cups tart apples (about 1 pound), peeled and cubed
- 1-1/2 cups pecan halves
- 1 cup golden raisins

> Sift dry ingredients together.
> In a large mixing bowl, beat oil, butter, sugar, eggs and vanilla until creamy.
> Stir in dry ingredients (batter will be very thick). Fold in apples, pecans and raisins.
> Spoon into a greased and floured 10-inch tube or bundt pan. Smooth out the top.
> Bake about 90 minutes at 350 degrees or until a toothpick inserted into the center comes out clean.
> Cool the cake completely in the pan. Then invert onto a platter and cut into wedges.

from **The Lansing House B&B**
291 Front Street
Lansing, Iowa 52151
319-538-4263

Innkeeper Margaret FitzGerald often serves this cake as dessert for breakfast, over which guests linger in the sunroom to watch the Mississippi River flow by. She suggests the cake for Thanksgiving dessert or an autumn party. "It's a marvelously rich and wonderful apple cake," she said. "It keeps very well and I often cut it in half and freeze half of it."

The travelers who stay in this 100-year-old B&B can't get much closer to the Mississippi River. Margaret and Chris FitzGerald's home is separated from the river only by a railroad track, and it's just to the side and below the picturesque Blackhawk Bridge to Wisconsin. Most Midwesterners think of Lansing as being Michigan's capital city, but this Iowa river town is just over the Minnesota border, nestled among the limestone bluffs. Two guest-rooms are available here for explorers of the river, its backwaters, island sandbars or wildlife refuges. Hiking, canoeing and hunting also are popular.

Carrot Cake with Silky Lemon Frosting

Ingredients:

3 cups flour
2 teaspoons baking soda
1 teaspoon cinnamon
1 teaspoon ginger
1/2 teaspoon salt
3 eggs
1-1/2 cups sugar
3/4 cup mayonnaise
1 16-ounce can crushed pineapple, drained (save the juice)
3 cups carrots, shredded
1 cup raisins
1 cup walnuts, chopped

Silky Lemon Frosting:
8 ounces cream cheese, softened
1/2 cup margarine
1 tablespoon lemon juice
1-1/2 cups powdered sugar

> In a medium bowl, mix together flour, spices, soda and salt.
> In a large bowl, beat eggs, sugar, mayonnaise, pineapple and 1/2 cup pineapple juice at medium speed until well blended.
> Gradually beat in the flour mixture. Then stir in carrots, raisins and nuts.
> Pour into two greased and floured loaf pans or a 9 x 13-inch cake pan.
> Bake at 350 degrees for 50-55 minutes.
> For Silky Lemon Frosting, beat all ingredients until fluffy. Frost the cooled cake and refrigerate.

from **The American House**
410 East Third Street
Morris, Minnesota 56267
612-589-4054

Innkeeper Karen Berget often serves this moist cake at luncheons she caters to small groups at her inn or as a special breakfast dessert.

Karen and Kyle opened their B&B in 1984 in this 1901 clapboard home, complete with stained glass windows and gingerbread trim. Having had 11 owners before the Bergets and been cut into a duplex, the home required major restoration work. In the process, they uncovered original stenciled walls in the dining room and a walnut and oak parquet floor. Upstairs, the three guest-rooms have handstenciling and are furnished with antiques.

Another American House recipe:
Grandma's Chocolate Pie, page 201

Light Chocolate Ambrosia Roll

Ingredients:

3 eggs
1 cup sugar
3/4 cup flour
1/4 cup cocoa
1/4 teaspoon baking soda
1/4 teaspoon salt
1/3 cup milk
1 teaspoon vanilla
Fresh fruit, sliced thinly (bananas, strawberries, peaches and/or raspberries)

Filling:
1/2 cup butter
2 cups powdered sugar
1 egg
1 teaspoon vanilla

> Beat eggs until light. Add sugar and beat until thick. Add milk and vanilla and blend.
> Sift dry ingredients and stir quickly into egg mixture.
> Pour into a well-greased jelly roll pan that has been lined with waxed paper. Spread batter evenly.
> Bake at 375 degrees for 15 minutes. Do not over-bake.
> Turn cake out onto a towel that has been well-dusted with powdered sugar. Remove the waxed paper and roll as you would a jelly roll. Cool.
> For the filling, beat all ingredients together.
> Unroll the cake and spread the filling to within 1/2-inch of the edges.
> Place the fruit over the filling and re-roll without the towel.
> Cover and chill. Slice with a very sharp knife. Serve with a dollop of real whipped cream, optional.

from **The Inn at Wildcat Mountain**
Highway 33
Ontario, Wisconsin 54651
608-337-4352

There's fruit in here, if you need a redeeming value to serve something this sinful before noon. Innkeeper Patricia Barnes calls it a favorite of hers, "wonderful for those who love chocolate -- even for breakfast!" Guests at the Inn at Wildcat Mountain can begin to work off their breakfasts by walking a block and renting a canoe on the Kickapoo River. Or the Elroy-Sparta State Bike Trail can be picked up only nine miles away. This inn is in the heart of Amish country, so it's also fun to stop at Amish farms to talk and buy bentwood hickory furniture, maple syrup or a quilt.

Other Inn at Wildcat Mountain recipes:
Mother's Fresh Rhubarb Cake, page 39
Creamy Fruit Dressing, page 108

Joan's Lazy Cake

Ingredients:

3 cups flour
2 cups sugar
1/3 cup cocoa
2 scant teaspoons baking soda
1/2 teaspoon salt
2 tablespoons white vinegar
2 teaspoons vanilla
3/4 cup vegetable oil
2 cups cold water
1/2 cup chocolate chips
1 to 2 teaspoons almond-flavored liqueur, optional

> In a 9 x 13-inch pan, sift together the flour, sugar, cocoa, baking soda and salt. Then stir in chocolate chips.
> Level the ingredients in the pan. Then make three holes.
> In Hole #1, add the vinegar.
> In Hole #2, add the vanilla.
> In Hole #3, add the vegetable oil.
> Add liqueur to water. "Now have fun pouring two cups cold water over all." Stir with a fork until the batter is well-mixed and smooth. Do not beat!
> Bake at 350 degrees about 40 minutes or until a toothpick inserted in the center comes out clean.

from **Seven Pines Lodge**
Lewis, Wisconsin 54851
715-653-2323

"It's even better the second day, if you can wait that long!" said Innkeeper Joan Simpson. Frosting is optional, and sprinkling with powdered sugar will satisfy most. Since her guests already may have ordered an unusual breakfast entree -- fresh trout -- they might as well continue with an untraditional breakfast and have a slice of this cake for dessert. Eating isn't all there is to do at Seven Pines. Many guests come to fish the private stocked trout stream. Others are happy to have Moses, the yellow Lab, lead them along the paths by the stream. In the winter, guests come in groups to x-c ski and enjoy the fieldstone fireplace. Five rooms are available in the main lodge and two in the carriage house.

Other Seven Pines Lodge recipes:
Trout Amandine, page 159
Blue Trout, page 160

Grandma's Custard Bread Pudding

Ingredients:

    4 eggs
    1/2 cup sugar
    2 cups milk
    1 cup buttermilk
    3 slices bread - whole wheat raisin bread or whole wheat walnut bread
    1 teaspoon pure vanilla extract (not imitation)
    1/2 cup raisins
    1/4 cup spiced rum

Also:

    Nutmeg
    Cinnamon

> Heat the rum (available at liquor stores) and soak the raisins in it until the rum has cooled again.

> Beat the eggs, sugar and milk together.

> Pulverize the bread to fine crumbs in a food processor. Add to the egg mixture.

> Stir in the raisins. Pour the mixture into a 1-1/2-quart glass baking dish. Sprinkle with nutmeg and cinnamon.

> Fill a larger pan with hot water about one-inch deep. Then place the baking dish in it.

> Bake uncovered for one hour at 350 degrees.

from **The Hutchinson House**
305 Northwest Second Street
Faribault, Minnesota 55021
507-332-7519

Innkeeper Marilyn Coughlin has improved a little bit on Grandma's recipe. The hot spiced rum, for instance, plumps up the raisins. Combined with whole wheat bread and buttermilk, what could be ordinary bread pudding is anything but. She serves it as dessert for breakfast unless the entree has been French toast, pancakes or something heavy on the bread.

Guests here stay in one of four suite-sized rooms, decorated with antiques and imported goosedown comforters. The home has an octagonal turret with bullet holes at attic level where a previous owner practiced target shooting. Guests have a 1900s Victrola in the front parlor with stacks of old records to play and they may use the fireplace in the living room.

Other Hutchinson House recipes:
Celia's English Coconut Tea Loaf, page 73
Baked Stuffed Peaches, page 166

Pumpkin Custard Flan

Ingredients:

9 slices of bread (leftover caramel or cinnamon rolls work well)
3 tablespoons butter, melted
1-1/2 cups warm milk
1 cup of cooked or canned pumpkin
3 tablespoons molasses
3/4 cup brown sugar
3 eggs
1-1/2 teaspoons cinnamon
1 teaspoon vanilla
1/4 teaspoon salt
1/2 cup raisins, optional

Also:

Whipped topping or whipped cream

> Cut up bread or rolls. Place in a greased round cake pan or flan pan to three-quarters full.
> Mix the remaining ingredients and pour them over the bread.
> Bake at 350 degrees for 45-55 minutes. Turn out onto a serving plate.
> Pipe whipped cream around the flan.
> If you're making your own whipped topping: add 1 tablespoon instant coffee and 2 tablespoons powdered sugar to 1 cup dry whipped topping mix. Whip until stiff peaks form.

Makes 12 servings

from **The Rivertown Inn**
306 West Olive Street
Stillwater, Minnesota 55082
612-430-2955

This turns out to be a fancy breakfast dessert when the whipped cream topping is piped around the flan. Chuck and Judy Dougherty might serve it on weekdays, as dessert after breakfast entrees, or as part of their hearty weekend breakfast buffet, with more than a dozen kinds of pastries fresh out of the oven, and fruit and cheese. Guests can choose to come down to breakfast in the large dining room or wrap-around screened porch, or the Doughertys will bring breakfast trays to their rooms. As caterers, the Doughertys also offer pre-arranged luncheons, dinners and teas.

Other Rivertown Inn recipes:
Danish Kringle, page 35
Eggs Mornay, page 121
Blueberry Buttermilk Oatmeal Pancakes, page 131

Innkeepers know that food can be a symbol of hospitality and can help a guest to feel at home. Many innkeepers don't wait for breakfast the next morning to put their guests at ease. A social hour in the parlor or on the porch often includes appetizers or sweets. Some innkeepers leave a bedtime snack by the bed or by the fireplace. Others have a cookie jar open on a help-yourself basis. At least one innkeeper prepares a going-away gift for first-time guests. It's easy to see why they want to share these great recipes for their "other favorites!"

Other Favorites

Fantastic Brownies

Ingredients:

1/2 cup butter, melted
1 cup sugar
2 eggs
1 teaspoon vanilla
1 cup walnuts or pecans, chopped
1/2 cup flour
1/8 teaspoon baking powder
2 squares unsweetened chocolate, melted

Also:

Powdered sugar

> Cream together sugar, eggs, butter, vanilla and melted chocolate.
> Add dry ingredients.
> Pour into a greased 8 x 8 x 2-inch pan.
> Bake at 325 degrees for 30 minutes. Cool and sprinkle with powdered sugar.

from **Silver Creek B&B**
4361 U.S. Highway 23 South
Black River, Michigan 48721
517-471-2198

This simple, sinful recipe was given to Innkeeper Kim Moses by her mother-in-law, and chocoholics will attest it proves the stuff out of a boxed mix is nothing like "scratch" brownies.

These brownies are one of the homemade treats guests will find set out in the pantry and available anytime, day or night, along with hot coffee. Kim suggests they pour themselves a cup, grab a couple brownies and sit down to listen to an old recording of Nelson Eddy, played on an antique phonograph, constructed before RCA Victor received its patent. As an antique collector and dealer, Kim gives guests a tour of the home, which has five guest rooms, and she can answer questions about all the antique pieces.

Other Silver Creek B&B recipes:
English Muffin Loaf, page 76
Pecan Pull-Apart Sticky Buns, page 86
Michigan Fruit Cup with Pecan Sauce, page 112
Pecan Waffles, page 145

Grandma's Chocolate Pie

Ingredients:

1/2 cup margarine or butter, at room temperature
3/4 cup sugar
1 teaspoon vanilla
1 ounce unsweetened liquid chocolate
2 eggs, at room temperature
1 baked 8 or 9-inch pie shell

> Beat the margarine, sugar, vanilla and chocolate.
> Add one egg and beat well.
> Add the second egg and beat well.
> Continue beating -- "The trick is to beat long enough (about 20 minutes) until all the sugar granules are dissolved."
> Fold into a pie shell and freeze overnight.

from **The American House**
410 East Third Street
Morris, Minnesota 56267
612-589-4054

"As a child, I always looked forward to Grandma's visits because that always meant wonderful aromas would soon be coming from the ktichen," said Innkeeper Karen Berget. "A favorite of the whole family was her chocolate pie. We always fought over the last piece!"

Today Karen has wonderful aromas coming from her own kitchen in this 1901 house. Karen is a native of Stillwater, which is Minnesota's birthplace and the site of a number of glorious old homes and fine B&Bs. When she and Kyle moved to Morris, this house reminded her of Stillwater and when they toured it, they thought it would make a good B&B. After months of renovation and research, they opened three guest-rooms upstairs. Karen also runs a catering business in the home.

The guest-room walls are handstenciled, handmade quilts are on the antique beds, and guests have a room upstairs for television and games. A bicycle-built-for-two is ready for guests who want to take a riding tour of Morris, home of one of the University of Minnesota campuses.

Another American House recipe:
Carrot Cake with Silky Lemon Frosting, page 194

Crispy Caramel Corn

Ingredients:
- 1/2 cup sugar
- 1/4 cup (4 tablespoons) margarine
- 1/2 cup dark corn syrup
- 1/2 teaspoon vanilla
- 1/2 teaspoon salt
- 2 quarts popped popcorn

> Cook the above ingredients, except popcorn, at medium-high heat for five minutes, stirring constantly. This is to dissolve the sugar and create a light syrup.
> In a very large bowl, mix the caramel with the popcorn.
> Bake in a jelly roll pan at 250 degrees for one hour, stirring every 15 minutes.
> Cool in the pan, still stirring occasionally.

Microwave option:
> Put the caramel-coated corn in a clean brown grocery bag. Fold the top over a couple times to seal, and then shake the bag.
> Microwave on high setting for one minute, then shake the bag. Microwave again for one minute, shake the bag. Microwave a third time for 30 seconds. Be careful not to overcook. Remove popcorn to a serving bowl and cool.
> Note that this method is faster, but the caramel corn is not as crisp as with the oven method.

from **The Inn at
Cedar Crossing**
**336 Louisiana Street
Sturgeon Bay, Wisconsin 54235
414-743-4200**

"One of the treats we serve our guests before the evening fire is caramel corn," said Innkeeper Terry Wulf, who insists on using only the oven method for her caramel corn. Guests at this country inn in the city have a lounge area with a fireplace upstairs. Guests from all nine rooms can meet and enjoy the caramel corn, which invaribly leads to swapping stories about Door County adventures and recalling the last time they had really good, homemade caramel corn.

Other Inn at Cedar Crossing recipes:
Apple Yogurt Coffeecake, page 30
Surpise Muffins, page 58
Fresh Rhubarb Bread, page 84
Zucchini Chocolate Nut Bread, page 88
Nectarines with Cream Anglaise, page 113
Hot Apple Crisp, page 192

Currant News Pie

Ingredients:
Dough for a two-crust pie
4 cups fresh currants
2/3 cup, more or less, sugar
1/4 cup flour
1-1/2 tablespoons lemon juice
1-1/2 tablespoons butter

Also:
Almond-flavored liqueur
Vanilla ice cream

> Wash and drain currants. Add lemon juice, then sugar and flour. Stir gently to blend. Let the mixture stand for 15 minutes.
> Roll out the two crusts. Line a pie pan with one crust and sprinkle flour lightly on the bottom.
> Pour the currant mixture into the pie shell. Dot with butter. Cover with second crust, seal the edges and prick the top.
> Bake at 450 degrees for 10 minutes. Then reduce heat to 350 and bake for 35 minutes, until the pie crust is golden brown.
> Serve with vanilla ice cream drizzled with a touch of almond-flavored liqueur.

from **Victorian Treasure B&B**
115 Prairie Street
Lodi, Wisconsin 53555
608-592-5199

"After I 'discovered' currants at the Madison Farmer's Market, I was determined to find a use for them other than jelly," said Innkeeper Linda Bishop. "This pie more than fit the bill." She serves it to summer guests on the wrap-around veranda of this 1897 home.

Currants have not been the only discovery she and husband Joe Costanza have made since moving to Wisconsin. Their home was a discovery in itself, with an unusual amount of original elegant fixtures and woodwork, including cypress. The Lodi area has been another discovery that they like to share. The B&B is close to Wisconsin River activities and other outdoor activities like hiking and rock climbing in the "Baraboo Range."

Another Victorian Treasure B&B recipe:
Broiled Sunshine, page 106

Finnish Cakes

Ingredients:
>2 tablespoons margarine
>3 eggs, beaten
>1/4 to 1/2 cup sugar
>2 cups milk
>1 cup flour
>Dash of salt

Also:
>Powdered sugar

> In a large jelly roll pan, put 2 tablespoons margarine (or 1 tablespoon each in two round pizza pans). Place the pan(s) in the oven, preheating to 400 degrees. Melt but do not brown the margarine and turn to coat the bottom of the pan(s).
> Mix eggs, sugar, milk, flour and salt. Pour over the margarine.
> Bake at 400 degrees for 25-30 minutes.
> Remove from the oven and sprinkle with powdered sugar. Cut in wedges and serve warm.

Makes up to 6 servings per pan

from **The Inn**
Wisconsin Avenue
Montreal, Wisconsin 54550
715-561-5180

"My dear friend Hilma Auguston, a Finlander and I think the best cook on the Wisconsin Iron Range, makes this for us to have with our afternoon coffee," said Innkeeper Doree Schumacher. These thin wedges are so sweet they need no other topping than powdered sugar.

Guests at The Inn may eat these cakes during an aprés-ski hour by the fireplace after a day on the slopes or trails in this big snow country. After operating a private alpine ski school, Doree and Dick converted this former mining headquarters building into a B&B with three suites. One of the suites includes a third floor loft in the mine's former chemistry labs and the lab table with sink is still in place.

Wisconsin and Michigan state parks are nearby, and the Hurley-Ironwood area is well known for summer recreation, plus fall color touring.

Another Inn recipe:
Cottage Cheese Blender Pancakes, page 135

Fresh Fruit Pizza

Ingredients:

 1 cup flour
 1/2 cup butter
 1/4 cup powdered sugar
 1 8-ounce package cream cheese
 1/3 cup plus 1/2 cup sugar
 1 teaspoon vanilla
 1 cup pineapple juice
 1 teaspoon lemon juice
 2 tablespoons cornstarch
 1 20-ounce can pineapple rings
 2 to 4 kinds of seasonal fruit

> For the crust, mix the flour, butter and powdered sugar. Press the crust into a pizza pan or a 9 x 13-inch jelly roll pan.
> Bake at 325 degrees for 15 minutes, then cool.
> For the filling, mix cream cheese, 1/3 cup sugar and vanilla.
> Spread the filling on the cooled crust.
> For the glaze, mix the pineapple juice, 1/2 cup sugar, lemon juice and cornstarch in a saucepan. Cook until the mixture is thick. Cool.
> Drain the pineapple rings. Wash and slice the other fruit. Arrange it over the filling.
> Pour cooled glaze over the fruit. (When using bananas or peaches, make sure the glaze completely covers the slices because it prevents the fruit from discoloring.)
> Keep refrigerated. Serve with whipped cream, optional.

from **Evergreen Knoll Acres**
Country Bed & Breakfast
Rural Route 1, Box 145
Lake City, Minnesota 55041
612-345-2257

Many of Bev and Paul Meyer's guests will eat dinner at a restaurant and then save room for a slice of Bev's Fresh Fruit Pizza before bed. This recipe is one of Bev's favorites for summertime, when a lot of fresh fruit can be used. "I usually start with drained pineapple rings and add whatever is in season. Strawberries, bananas and kiwi fruit are a favorite." She also likes a pineapple-peach-blueberry-kiwi combination.

Other Evergreen Knoll Acres recipes:
Streusel Coffeecake, page 42
Aunt Clara's Strawberry Jam, page 99
Strawberry Cheddar Cheesecake, page 179

Grandma Joan's Gingersnaps

Ingredients:

  1 cup shortening
  1 cup sugar
  2/3 cup molasses
  2/3 cup hot coffee
  5 cups flour
  1/2 teaspoon salt
  1 teaspoon baking soda
  1 teaspoon ginger
  1/2 teaspoon cloves
  1/2 teaspoon cinnamon

> Cream shortening with sugar.
> Add hot coffee to the molasses. Then beat into the creamed sugar.
> In a separate bowl, sift together dry ingredients.
> Stir dry ingredients into the molasses mixture.
> The dough is very soft. Refrigerate three hours.
> Roll the chilled dough to 1/8-inch thickness on a floured board.
> Cut into shapes with a cookie cutter. Place cookies on an ungreased cookie sheet.
> Bake at 350 degrees for 10-12 minutes.
> Frost with icing and decorate, if desired.

Makes 9 dozen

from **Grandma Joan's Homestay**
2204 Brett Drive
Champaign, Illinois 61821
217-356-5828

Innkeeper Joan Erickson, otherwise known as "Grandma Joan," believes in "grandmothering" her B&B guests, including cookies and milk at bedtime. This is a family recipe that reflects her German heritage. She reports she gets nothing but compliments on this bedtime snack.

Joan's two-story contemporary home is located in southwest Champaign, home of the University of Illinois. Visitors staying in the four guest-rooms are welcome to use the family room and to enjoy a James Dean movie from her tape collection. Breakfast may include an item from her large backyard garden, and she often sends a "garden gift" home with guests.

Jan Hägel

Ingredients:

- 1 cup butter
- 1 cup sugar
- 1 egg yolk
- 2 cups flour
- 1/2 teaspoon cinnamon
- 1/2 cup walnuts, chopped

> Mix the butter, sugar and egg yolk.
> In a separate bowl, mix the flour and cinnamon. Then stir it into the butter mixture.
> Pat the batter into a greased 9 x 13-inch pan. Sprinkle with nuts.
> Bake at 350 degrees for 20-25 minutes.
> Cut immediately into bars.

from **The Comfort Guest House**
1000 Third Street
Galena, Illinois 61036
815-777-3062

"I can stir this bar up in 10 minutes and join my guests on the front porch with sun tea, and in 20 minutes everyone has a Swedish treat," said Innkeeper Connie Sola. "They're also wonderful with coffee in front of the fireplace on a cool October evening."

Guests at this 1856 home especially enjoy the porch swing and the vegetable and perennial gardens. Connie is one of the master gardeners in the area and she often trades seeds and loves talking growing tips over breakfast. Breakfast may include some garden produce, and it's served in the formal dining room at the family oak table, set with her grandmother's silver. The three guest-rooms are filled with antiques and hand-tied quilts.

Downtown Galena is only four blocks away. Visitors have discovered the restored river town, just 20 miles from Dubuque, and come to shop the antique and gift shops, buy handmade candy, take historic walking tours, or just gawk at the outstanding examples of 1800s architecture, from elaborate mansions to the humble homes of the region's lead miners.

Old-Fashioned Lemon Curd Tart Filling

Ingredients:
>   3 whole eggs
>   3 egg yolks
>   1 cup sugar
>   1/2 cup lemon juice, fresh-squeezed
>   4 tablespoons butter, melted
>   Rind of a whole lemon, finely chopped

> In a glass bowl, beat together the eggs, yolks, sugar and lemon juice. Beat well with a whisk.
> Beat in the butter and lemon rind.
> Place the bowl in the microwave. Heat on "high" for 1-1/2 minutes. (Or cook until thick in a double boiler over medium heat.)
> Remove from the microwave and beat well.
> Heat again for 1-1/2 minutes.
> Remove again and beat well.
> Microwave for a third time for 1-1/2 minutes.
> Remove again and beat well. By this time, the lemon curd should be silky smooth and thickened.
> Cover with plastic wrap and refrigerate.

Makes about 2 cups

from **The Redstone Inn**
504 Bluff Street
Dubuque, Iowa 52001
319-582-1894

Lemon curd might be old-fashioned, but the microwave has considerably improved the cooking method. "This tart filling is used for the Redstone's English Tea Plate and is also good for a larger tart or pie filling, topped with whipped cream," said Manager Debbie Griesinger. Once it's in the refrigerator, it's easy to find other uses, such as a topping for cheesecake, gingerbread or waffles (whipped cream can be a topping over the topping).

The Redstone Inn is one of Dubuque's grandest structures, a huge Victorian mansion built for the 1894 wedding of the daughter of the Cooper Wagon Works owner. Ninety years later, 17 Dubuque investors began restoration of the old home, and 15 rooms opened in 1985. The guest-rooms are all different and furnished with antiques found within 100 miles of Dubuque. The mansion's dining room serves afternoon English Tea to the public, a popular event, and caters private parties and special events.

Naughty Torte

Ingredients:

4 ounces semi-sweet chocolate
4 ounces peanut butter chips
2 sticks (1 cup) butter
1-1/4 cups sugar
6 large eggs

Also:

Whipped cream
Cocoa for sprinkling

> Butter a 9 x 1-1/2 inch round cake pan. Cut and place a buttered piece of waxed paper or parchment on the bottom.
> In a double boiler, melt the chocolate and peanut butter chips.
> Add butter. Stir until the mixture is smooth.
> Slowly stir in sugar.
> In another bowl, beat eggs until they are foamy. Mix eggs into the chocolate-sugar mixture.
> Pour into the prepared pan. Place it in a larger pan. Add water to the larger pan to come half-way up the side of the cake pan.
> Bake in the center of a 350-degree oven for 90 minutes.
> Cool for five minutes. Then invert onto a serving plate and remove waxed paper or parchment. Serve chilled or at room temperature with whipped cream and a little cocoa sprinkled on top for decoration.

Cut in 16 small, rich slices

from **Hannah Marie
Country Inn**
Route 1, Highway 71 South
Spencer, Iowa 51301
712-262-1286

Sweet treats like this are one of the features at special teas that Mary and Ray Nichols and their son, David, host at this inn in rural Iowa. Ray begins the teas with open-faced sandwiches and, of course, tea and coffee. Then comes a course of baked goods, such as scones, tarts and English tea breads. This super-rich torte is served in small slices for dessert.

Renovating and opening this inn has hardly been retirement for Mary and Ray. After opening three guest-rooms, they began serving teas as many as six days a week. The inn is open June through November each year.

Other Hannah Marie Country Inn recipes:
Mary's Elbows, page 26
Three Pepper Frittata, page 152

Chilled Pineapple Peach Soup

Ingredients:

    1-1/2 pounds fresh peaches
    Half a fresh pineapple
    1 cup fresh-squeezed orange juice
    1 cup pineapple juice
    2 cups plain yogurt
    1/2 cup dry white wine
    1 tablespoon fresh lemon juice

Also:

    Lime slices and mint leaves

> Peel, pit and slice the peaches. Then purée the peaches and pineapple in a food processor or blender. The mixture should be smooth.
> Add juices, yogurt and wine and blend well.
> Pass the soup through a fine strainer.
> Serve chilled with thin slices of lime and mint leaves.

Makes 8 servings

from **The Old Holland Inn**
133 West 11th Street
Holland, Michigan 49423
616-396-6601

This recipe was inspired by a Caribbean breakfast, said Innkeeper Dave Plaggemars. He and Fran met at Negril, Jamaica, and they love the tropics and like to bring a bit home to Holland, a city with an international flavor of its own. They serve the soup "as an afternoon refresher for guests returning from a hard day at the beaches of Lake Michigan," Dave said.

Their B&B is located just a few minutes drive from Saugatuck and other spots on the great lake, and within walking distance of Lake Macatawa and downtown Holland. That's a big plus during the town's annual festival, Tulip Time, in early May. Their location is a plus the rest of the year, as well, since nearby Hope College has groomed x-c ski trails and there are another 30 miles of trails in the vicinity. Since they opened in 1986, the world has, indeed, beat a path to their door. They've hosted guests from 35 states and 17 countries with their brand of Midwest hospitality.

Other Old Holland Inn recipes:
Whole Wheat Apple Nut Oatmeal Muffins, page 45
Poppy Seed Orange Date-Nut Bread, page 75
Poached Pears in Cranapple Juice, page 115

Nine Bean Soup

Ingredients:

2 cups Nine Bean Soup Mix
2 quarts water
1 pound cooked ham, cubed
1 large onion, diced
1 clove garlic, minced
1 teaspoon salt
1 16-ounce can tomatoes, undrained and chopped
1 10-ounce can tomatoes and green chiles, undrained

Nine Bean Soup Mix:
Navy beans
Pinto beans
Red kidney beans
Black-eyed peas
Barley
Black beans
Split green peas
Split yellow peas
Baby lima beans

> Sort and wash bean mix (mixed in your favorite proportions), then place in a Dutch oven.
> Cover the beans with water (it should be two inches above dry beans). Let soak overnight.
> The next day, drain the beans. Add the water, ham, onion, garlic and salt.
> Cover and bring the mixture to a boil.
> Reduce heat and simmer 60-90 minutes or until the beans are tender.
> Stir in the two types of tomatoes. Simmer 30 minutes more, stirring occasionally.

Makes 8 cups

from **The Arman House**
2581 Grove Street
Boyne Falls, Michigan 49713
616-549-2764

A calico-covered jar of this Nine Bean Soup Mix, with the recipe tucked inside, is a gift to all first-time guests. "Guests are encouraged to keep the jar in their kitchens, pass it on to friends, even make the soup -- it's delicious -- and return for a refill," said Innkeeper Jackie Arman. Leaving with a little gift is part of the hospitality in this 19th century home.

Jackie and Norm Arman have had hospitality on their minds since opening their B&B in 1986. Jackie hand-stenciled the walls of the three guest-rooms, and the crafts were made by her or friends. Guests are invited to enjoy the property, including a babbling brook running through the yard. Armans point them to Boyne Mountain Ski Resort, located nearby, golf courses, swimming beaches, x-c trails, good restaurants, and they'll even give general hints on where to hunt morels in the spring.

Another Arman House recipe:
Crustless Potato Quiche, page 124

Sourdough Crackers (Lavosch)

<u>Ingredients:</u>

4 cups bubbling sourdough (A recipe is on page 41. If none, double yeast)
1 package dry yeast
1 cup warm water
1 teaspoon sugar
1/4 cup (4 tablespoons) margarine, melted and cooled
1 tablespoon salt
2-1/2 to 3-1/2 cups flour, unsifted

> Mix sugar in water. Add yeast and stir to dissolve.
> Mix salt and one cup of the flour into the 4 cups sourdough.
> Add the sugar-yeast mixture and margarine to the sourdough. Use the electric mixer, adding flour and mixing until the motor heats up and dough becomes stiff.
> Dump the stiff dough onto a floured board. Keep on adding flour "until the dough resembles a baby's bottom or an earlobe - the cookbooks call it 'smooth and elastic.' "
> Put the dough into a buttered, non-metal bowl to rise. Turn the dough to butter the top and cover. Let the dough rise in a warm place, free from drafts, until doubled in size, one to two hours.
> Punch down the dough. Divide it into eight equal pieces and cover six with inverted bowl.
> Roll out two pieces at a time and then stretch them to resemble a thin pizza crust.
> Poke them all over with a fork and place on ungreased cookie sheets.
> Bake at 325 degrees for about 20 minutes until golden brown.
> Cool and break into cracker-sized pieces. Serve with cheeses, patés, etc. Store in an air-tight container.

from **The Canterbury Inn**
723 Second Street SW
Rochester, Minnesota 55902
507-289-5553

"We developed this recipe in order to use our sourdough starter more frequently than we did while making regular sourdough bread," said Innkeeper Mary Martin. Five kinds of bread are baked here and kept on hand in the freezer, but still, one type wasn't enough use for sourdough. "Our sourdough starter was passed along from a friend whose family had been using and tending it for some 30 years," and it's reportedly from a real Alaskan "sourdough." These crackers frequently are served at the inn's bountiful tea from 5:30 to 7 every night.

Other Canterbury Inn recipes:
Pesto, page 97
Canterbury Eggs Benedict, page 119
Minnesota Wild Rice Waffles, page 144

Tomato Bites

Ingredients:

Ripe tomatoes, sliced 1/2 to 3/4-inches thick (home-grown are best)
Parmesan, Romano, cheddar and/or Muenster cheeses, grated
Garlic salt
Crisp cooked bacon, crumbled

Also:

Favorite spices, such as basil or dill

> Sprinkle any combination of cheeses on top of the tomato slices.
> Add on garlic salt (and any other favorite spice or seasoning).
> Top with crumbled, crisp bacon.
> Broil for about five minutes or until warmed through but still firm.

from **The Scanlan House**
708 Parkway South
Lanesboro, Minnesota 55949
507-467-2158

Innkeeper Mary Mensing may serve hot slices of fresh tomatoes to summer guests as appetizers. "These are fast and do not cause a lot of extra work but add a nice touch to your meal or afternoon appetizers," she said.

In the summer, despite the appeal of this 1889 Victorian home, it's unlikely to find many guests indoors for very long. The Lanesboro area is full of recreational opportunities that draw many Twin Citians (about a three-hour drive), yet it retains small-town appeal. The state maintains the Root River Trail, used for hiking and biking in the summer and x-c skiing in the winter. Also, the Department of Natural Resources' fish hatchery is two miles away and open to visitors. The Root River itself is a fine trout river. It's also a popular canoeing and innertubing river, and the Mensing family will help guests make arrangements for equipment rentals.

Visitors also are interested in a local Amish settlement, a winery and guided cave tours in the limestone bluff region, Mensings report. They also recommend visiting the Forest Resource Center for its educational programs and wooded hiking trails.

Another Scanlan House recipe:
Cinnamon Raisin Biscuits, page 65

Contents by Inn

MICHIGAN

MINNESOTA

American House, Morris
Carrot Cake with Silky Lemon Frosting - Dessert for Breakfast, 194
Grandma's Chocolate Pie - Other Favorites, 201

Bluff Creek Inn, Chaska
Candlelight Coffee for Two - Beverages, 22
Stuffed Baked Apples - Fruits, 103
Special Valentine Meringues - Holiday Fare, 189

Canterbury Inn, Rochester
Pesto - Preserves, Butters, Spreads and Sauces, 97
Canterbury Eggs Benedict - Entrees, 119
Minnesota Wild Rice Waffles - Entrees, 144
Sourdough Crackers (Lavosch) - Other Favorites, 212

Carrolton Country Inn, Lanesboro
Summer Sherbet Tea - Beverages, 27

Cedar Knoll Farm, Good Thunder
Golden Fruit Cup - Fruits, 110
Frau Paquin's Egg Roll-Ups - Go-Alongs, 163

Chase's, Spring Valley
Corn Pancakes - Entrees, 134

Country Bed & Breakfast, Shafer
Swedish Egg Coffee - Beverages, 23

Driscoll's for Guests, Stillwater
Cider to Sit Around With - Beverages, 20
Pumpkin Poundcake - Breads, 83
Oo-Hoo's Strawberry-Rhubarb Jam - Preserves, Butters, Spreads and Sauces, 100

Eden B&B, Dodge Center
Apple Bran Muffins - Muffins, 46

Evergreen Knoll Acres, Lake City
Streusel Coffee Cake - Coffeecakes, 42
Aunt Clara's Strawberry Preserves - Preserves, Butters, Spreads and Sauces, 99
Strawberry Cheddar Cheesecake - Holiday Fare, 179
Fresh Fruit Pizza - Dessert for Breakfast, 205

Hutchinson House, Faribault
Celia's English Coconut Tea Loaf - Breads, 73
Baked Stuffed Peaches - Go-Alongs, 166
Grandma's Custard Bread Pudding - Dessert for Breakfast, 197

Traveling to these B&Bs?

Before heading out, contact the following state travel offices for maps and publications:

Illinois
Illinois Tourist Information Center
310 South Michigan Ave., Suite 108
Chicago, IL 60604
312-793-2094
1-800-223-0121

Iowa
Iowa Bureau of Visitors and Tourism
200 East Grand Ave.
Des Moines, IA 50309
515-281-3100
1-800-345-IOWA

Michigan
Michigan Travel Bureau
P.O. Box 30226
Lansing, MI 48909
1-800-5432-YES

Minnesota
Minnesota Office of Tourism
250 Skyway Level
375 Jackson Street
St. Paul, MN 55101
From Outside Minnesota: 1-800-328-1461
From Instate Minnesota: 1-800-652-9747
From the Twin Cities: 296-5029

Wisconsin
Wisconsin Division of Tourism
123 W. Washington Ave.
P.O. Box 7970
Madison, WI 53707
1-800-432-TRIP for a travel planner only
1-800-ESCAPES for vacation information and publications

Ordering Information

Traveling to Minnesota? Minnesota's best historic B&Bs are included in **Room at the Inn/Minnesota - Guide to Minnesota's Historic B&Bs, Hotels and Country Inns.**
The book includes an exterior photo of each establishment, plus information on the history of the inn, rooms, rates, policies on pets, smoking, children, deposits and payment, driving times from the Twin Cities, and more.
    Cost: $9.95 retail, plus $2.00 postage, handling and tax = $11.95

Room at the Inn/Wisconsin - Guide to Wisconsin's Historic B&Bs and Country Inns makes a great gift for all travelers, with photos and information on 86 establishments.
    Cost: $9.95 retail, plus $2.00 postage, handling and tax = $11.95

Additional copies of **Wake Up and Smell the Coffee** may be ordered by mail.
    Cost: $12.95 retail, plus $2.00 postage handling and tax = $14.95

TO ORDER BY PHONE using a credit card, call Voyageur Press in Stillwater, Minn.:
    1-800-888-9653 toll-free, or **612-430-2210.**

TO ORDER BY MAIL, send a check to **Down to Earth Publications, 1426 Sheldon, St. Paul, MN 55108.** Please make checks payable to Down to Earth Publications.

- -

Mail Order Form

Mail to: **Down to Earth Publications**
         1426 Sheldon
         St. Paul, MN 55108

Please send me _____ **Room at the Inn/Minnesota** at $11.95 each.

Please send me _____ **Room at the Inn/Wisconsin** at $11.95 each.

Please send me _____ **Wake Up and Smell the Coffee** at $14.95 each.

I have enclosed $_____ for _____ book(s). Send it/them to:

Name: _____

Street: _____ Apt. No. _____

City: _____ State: _____ Zip: _____

About the author

Laura Zahn discovered the wonderful "Breakfast" part of "Bed & Breakfast" when traveling the backroads of Minnesota and Wisconsin to write her "Room at the Inn/Minnesota" and "Room at the Inn/Wisconsin" guidebooks to historic B&Bs and country inns.

She is president of Down to Earth Publications, a St. Paul, Minnesota, writing, publishing and public relations firm specializing in travel. Her travelwriting has appeared in many newspapers and magazines, including the Chicago Sun-Times, Dallas Morning News, Detroit News, Los Angeles Times, Milwaukee Journal, St. Paul Pioneer Press Dispatch, Star Tribune of the Twin Cities and Mpls.-St. Paul Magazine. Zahn has worked in public relations in Minnesota and as a reporter and editor on newspapers in Alaska and Minnesota.

"Wake Up and Smell the Coffee" is her fourth book. In addition to the two "Room at the Inn" guides, she is co-author and co-publisher of "Ride Guide to the Historic Alaska Railroad."

A native of Saginaw, Michigan, she passed a written test to win the "Betty Crocker Homemaker of the Year" award in high school and says, "Now I've finally done something remotely related, besides tour the Betty Crocker kitchens." She graduated from Northern Michigan University in Marquette. She shares her St. Paul home with Jim Miller, her geologist husband, and Kirby Puckett Zahn Miller, who was proudly adopted from the Humane Society of Ramsey County on the day the Minnesota Twins won the American League pennant in 1987.